GLENN OWEN

QuickBooks® Online
FOR ACCOUNTING

GLENN OWEN

QuickBooks® Online
FOR ACCOUNTING

CENGAGE
Learning®

Australia • Brazil • Mexico • Singapore • United Kingdom • United States

CENGAGE Learning®

QuickBooks® Online For Accounting
Glenn Owen

Vice President, General Manager, Science,
Math & Quantitative Business: Balraj Kalsi

Product Director: Mike Schenk

Product Manager: Jason Guyler

Content Developer: Andrea Meyer

 Production Assistant: Trisha Makley

 Senior Marketing Manager: Robin LeFevre

Senior Marketing Coordinator:
Eileen Corcoran

Art and Cover Direction, Production
Management, and Composition:
Cenveo Publisher Services

Intellectual Property

 Analyst: Brittani Morgan

 Project Manager: Betsy Hathaway

Manufacturing Planner: Doug Wilke

Cover Image(s): derrrek/Getty Images

For product information and technology assistance, contact us at
Cengage Learning Customer & Sales Support, 1-800-354-9706

For permission to use material from this text or product, submit all requests online at **www.cengage.com/permissions**
Further permissions questions can be emailed to
permissionrequest@cengage.com

Tables containing IRS withholding information/instructions is © 2013 and can be found at http://www.irs.gov/.

QuickBooks® software screenshots are courtesy of Quicken® © 2015 Cengage Learning.

Video icon © Nickylarson974/Shutterstock.com.

Library of Congress Control Number: 2015955693

ISBN: 978-1-305-95031-3

Cengage Learning
20 Channel Center Street
Boston, MA 02210
USA

Cengage Learning is a leading provider of customized learning solutions with employees residing in nearly 40 different countries and sales in more than 125 countries around the world. Find your local representative at **www.cengage.com**.

Cengage Learning products are represented in Canada by Nelson Education, Ltd.

To learn more about Cengage Learning Solutions, visit
www.cengage.com

Purchase any of our products at your local college store or at our preferred online store **www.cengagebrain.com**

Printed in the United States of America
Print Number: 01   Print Year: 2015

Brief Contents

360192

Contents

Preface

Overview

Accounting has arrived in the Cloud and its time has come. Cloud computing is a general term for anything that involves delivering hosted services over the Internet. According to a recent study by KPMG (a global network of professional firms), businesses large, medium, and small are using the Cloud to drive cost efficiencies, better enable a mobile workforce, and improve alignment with their customers and vendors.

Imagine being able to update your business's accounting information system from anywhere on any device using any operating system. That is where the global economy is going. Are you on the path?

Is this Text for You?

This text is for you if you are an instructor who desires a self-paced, self-directed environment for your students to learn the essentials of QuickBooks Online Plus (QBO) and review their understanding of financial accounting and reporting.

This text is for you if you are a business owner looking for a self-paced, self-directed environment for yourself to learn the essentials of QBO as well as a means to refresh your understanding of financial accounting and reporting.

This book focuses on QBO. It is not designed for users of QuickBooks Pro, Accountant, or any other desktop version of QuickBooks. In that case, my QuickBooks Accountant books are a better fit. The desktop version and online versions are different, and though you can import files created in the desktop version into the online version, significant differences exist as discussed in Chapter 1.

Instructional Design

Each chapter of this text begins with a listing of expected student learning outcomes followed by a step-by-step explanation of how to obtain those outcomes. In most chapters, the explanations utilize a Sample Company created by Intuit in which the author demonstrates how various operating, investing, and financing activities of a business are captured and then reported in QBO.

End of chapter questions, matching, and two student cases follow these explanations. The questions help you to review the text explained concepts and processes while the matching section helps with terms and definitions. The student cases provide the information necessary to add data to the student's company file. Each chapter requires the student to add information to the previous chapter's rendition. Thus, for success in learning, each student must complete the previous chapter's student case before attempting the next chapter's student case.

Each copy (license) of QBO will work with one and only one company other than the sample company provided online. In the author's other QuickBooks texts, multiple cases were available for illustration and practice. However, because of Intuit's limit of one company per license, that option was absent unless the user purchased multiple licenses, which was impractical and costly.

Solutions to each chapter's student case are provided in the instructor manual.

Textbook Goals

This textbook takes a user and a preparer perspective by illustrating how accounting information is created and then used for making decisions. QBO is user-friendly and provides point-can-click simplicity and sophisticated accounting reporting and analysis tools. The textbook uses proven and successful instructional design (described above) to demonstrate the application's features and elicit student interaction.

The first and foremost goal of this text is to help students review fundamental accounting concepts and principles through the use of the QBO application and the analysis of business events. The content of this text complements the first course in accounting principles or financial accounting. Thus this text should either be used concurrently with an accounting principles or financial accounting course or be used subsequent to completion of such a course.

A second goal of this text is to teach students how to set up QBO for a business, use it to record business events, and use it to generate financial statements and reports. Acquiring these skills will help students improve their job prospects whether the company they work for uses QuickBooks or not.

A third goal of this text is to teach students the value of a computerized accounting information system and how it can be used to communicate important information to business owners, investors, and creditors.

Date Warning

The Sample Company (created and maintained by Intuit) is used to demonstrate many aspects of QBO in this text. The author has no control over the dates used by Intuit and those dates may change depending on when you are accessing the file online. The dates which appear in the figures supplied by the author in this text may not be the dates which appear on your screen.

The student cases are set in 2018 and 2019. If transactions are entered into the student case in other than the proper period, answers will be wrong. Be careful entering dates into QBO when you are working on this case. The default date when entering new transactions into QBO is the computer's system date which may or may not be in 2018 or 2019.

Update Warning

QBO is frequently upgraded by Intuit to provide new features, correct errors, or improve functionality. This book was written in 2015 and all figures are based on how QBO looked at that time. If you are using this text in 2016 or later and Intuit has made modifications in how QBO looks and feels or functions, differences will occur, which are out of the author's control.

Instructor as Your Accountant

Your instructor may choose to have you assign him or her as your accountant so he or she can see your work and progress at his or her convenience without having you to "send" the file. In fact, you cannot "send" your file since all the files are on the Cloud. Instructions on how to set your instructor as your accountant are provided in Chapter 1.

Video Demonstrations

Video demonstrations are available throughout this text and are referenced by a Demonstration Icon in the margin. These demonstrations are stand-alone full-action videos with audio showing step-by-step illustrations of business processes explained in this text.

All of these are available via the text's companion web site located at http://www.cengagebrain.com. Navigate your browser to http://www.cengagebrain.com. Type Glenn Owen in the Search for Books or Materials text box, and then click Find. Locate and then click the QuickBooks Online text from the listing provided.

Click the Free Materials tab and then click Access Now. When you navigate your browser to the student companion site for the text, you should see Video Demonstrations. Video Demonstrations need to be downloaded from the companion site to your computer by clicking the Video Demonstrations text. Usually these files are downloaded to a folder on your computer called Downloads. In some cases you may be asked where you want these files downloaded.

The file you download is a very large compressed zip file. When you double-click the file downloaded you'll see a list of files. All of these need to be extracted (decompressed) first before you can view them. Click Extract to a folder and then create a folder on your computer or flash drive that you want to contain all of your demonstration files. Remember where you extracted these files so you can find them later.

About the Author

Glenn Owen is a tenured member of Allan Hancock College's Accounting and Business faculty, where he has lectured on accounting and information systems since 1995. In addition, he is a retired lecturer at the University of California at Santa Barbara, where he taught accounting and information systems courses from 1980 to 2011. His professional experience includes five years at Deloitte & Touche as well as vice president of finance positions at Westpac Resources, Inc., and Expertelligence, Inc. Mr. Owen is working on his 4th edition of his Using Excel and Access in Accounting text, which gives accounting students specific, self-paced instruction on the use of spreadsheets (Excel 2016) and database applications (Access 2016) in accounting. He has also recently completed the 14th edition of his QuickBooks Accountant for Accounting 2015 text, which is also a self-paced, case-based instruction on the use of a commercial accounting application (QuickBooks 2015). His innovative teaching style emphasizes the decision maker's perspective and encourages students to think creatively. His graduate studies in educational psychology and his 40 years of business experience yield a balanced blend of theory and practice.

Dedication

I would like to thank my wife Kelly for her support and assistance during the creation of this and previous editions of this text. Though our boys are out of the house and pursuing their own interests, she continues to listen to my often crazy ideas for new cases and experiences with college students, providing an excellent sounding board and reality check. You and the boys continue to define what life is all about.

Note to the Student and Instructor

The text and related data files created for this book were constructed using QuickBooks Online. In this version of QuickBooks Intuit continues its use of a basic payroll service but has made it more accessible by having it live on its Cloud-based system. QuickBooks Online initially comes with the current tax tables; however, these tables soon become outdated, and the payroll feature is disabled unless the user subscribes to the payroll service.

The author decided to use the manual payroll tax feature, which requires that students manually enter the tax deductions. This alleviates the discrepancies between the solutions manual and the students' data entry and removes the burden of having to purchase the tax table service for each copy of QuickBooks Online used. Instructions on how to set up payroll for manual calculation of payroll taxes are provided in the text. For more information, see your QuickBooks Online documentation.

All reports have a default feature that identifies the basis in which the report was created (e.g., accrual or cash) and the date and time the report was printed. The date and time shown on your report will, of course, be different from that shown in this text.

GLENN OWEN

QuickBooks® Online
FOR ACCOUNTING

An Introduction to QuickBooks Online Plus

1

Upon completion of this chapter, the students will be able to do the following:

- Identify the basic features of QuickBooks Online Plus (QBO)
- Explain how QBO is similar and differs from the desktop version of QuickBooks
- Create a new QBO account using codes provided with this text
- Provide information to QBO about your company
- Successfully navigate the QBO home page
- Assign their instructor as their "Accountant"
- Use QBO's help feature

Overview

The focus of this chapter is to introduce you to QBO and get your account and company established. A description of QBO will be provided along with a brief comparison of how QBO differs from its desktop version. This text includes codes, which will allow you to create your own personal account with Intuit and create one and only one company. You will assign your company a name which includes your name for identification purposes. Welcome to the journey.

What Is QBO?

QBO is an online version of the popular QuickBooks accounting software developed by Intuit. The software is designed to capture common business events like purchases from and payments to vendors, sales to and collections from customers, payments and receipts to/from other operating, investing, and financing activities, period end accrual adjustments, and reports. Reports include the standard financial statements, including the income statement, statement of stockholders' equity, balance sheet, statement of cash flows, and other useful reports like accounts receivable aging. All interaction with QBO is done via an Internet connection. In other words, if you have not connected to the Internet, you will have no QBO. In other words QBO cannot work off-line.

All interaction with QBO is done online, i.e., there are no files to maintain on a computer and everything is saved online. Thus, there is no need for backup files. The monthly fee for using QBO covers one and only one company. This text includes access codes for the user to create one company online for a limited amount of time.

How Is QBO Similar/Different than the Desktop Version QuickBooks?

Even though these two products share the name "QuickBooks", they are unrelated. QBO isn't a copy of QuickBooks that has been web-enabled. They are different products with different database structures and approaches to solving problems even though both were developed in-house by Intuit to capture and report on accounting events.

Not all features available in QBO are available in the Windows desktop version of QuickBooks Accountant (QBDT). Likewise, not all features of QBDT are available in QBO. QBO requires an Internet connection. QBDT requires installation of software on to a computer. QBO requires a monthly fee. QBDT requires a one-time purchase and no monthly fees.

A key difference is that because QBO is online, it works on multiple operating systems (Windows, Apple, etc.) and multiple devices (desktops, laptops, smart phones, or tablets). The same cannot be said for QBDT. Intuit requires different software for QBDT to run on a Windows-based or an Apple-based computer. In this text QBDT will always mean the Windows version of QuickBooks Accountant.

Some additional notable differences are the following:

- QBDT can be used for an unlimited number of companies; QBO limits you to one company per license fee. Need to manage more than one company using QuickBooks? Each will cost you another monthly fee.

- QBO can automatically download bank transactions for no additional cost.

- QBDT can track inventory purchases and sales based on an average cost assumption or a first-in-first-out assumption.

- QBO can track inventory purchases and sales only based on a first-in-first-out assumption.

- QBDT can account for the receipt of inventory items (receive items function) based on a purchase order, QBO cannot and calls inventory products and services.

- QBO can automatically schedule and send invoices while QBDT cannot.

- QBDT can perform manual payroll without paying Intuit a monthly payroll processing fee. QBO encourages you to sign up for its payroll service and makes manually processing payroll difficult.

- QBO can be accessed from anywhere in the world where you have access to the Internet. QBDT requires a computer with the QuickBooks application and data files installed.

- QBDT provides for profit and loss as well as balance sheet budgeting. QBO only provides for profit and loss budgeting.

- QBO operates irrespective of platform (desktop, laptop, mobile device, or tablet) or operating system (Microsoft Windows, Apple iOS). QBDT does have a version of QuickBooks for both of those operating systems but they are different and require two separate application purchases.

- QBDT includes a fixed asset management, which will calculate depreciation and maintain detailed fixed asset records by individual asset while QBO does not calculate depreciation and does not maintain detailed records of fixed assets.

- QBO provides automatic upgrades; this is a good and a bad feature. With QuickBooks Online, you are almost always running the most current version (whether you want to or not).

Creating a New QBO Account

Before getting started, you will need to establish your account with QBO. This text includes access codes for one user. Once you use the codes, they will not work again.

To launch QBO and create a new account, do the following:

1   Open your Internet browser.

2   Type **https://quickbooks.intuit.com/start/retail_sui** into your browser's address text box.

3   Type your license number and product number (provided with the text) shown in Figure 1.1.

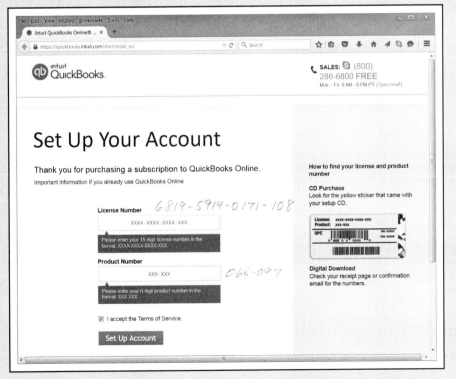

Figure 1.1

Set Up Your Account window

4   Click the **I accept the Terms of Service** check box and then click **Set Up Account**.

5   Enter information about you as shown in Figure 1.2 changing all the information to your name, your email, your id, and your password.

Figure 1.2

Setting Up Your Account

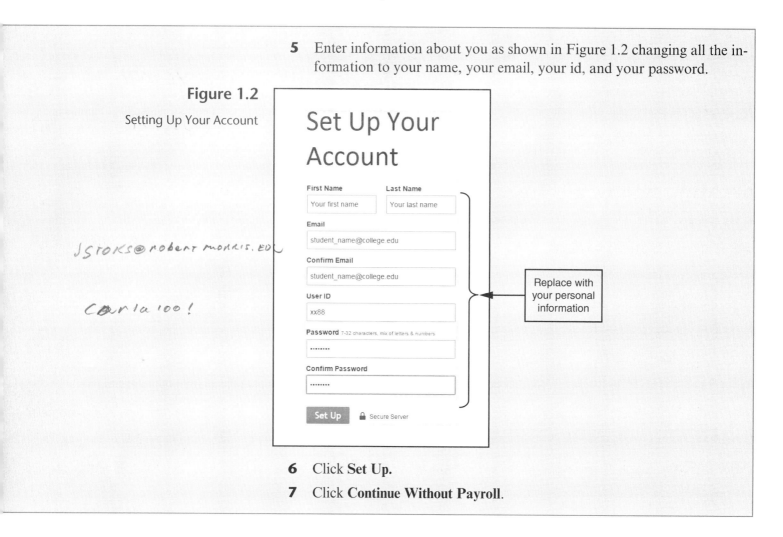

JSTOKS@robert morris.edu

Carla 100!

6   Click **Set Up.**

7   Click **Continue Without Payroll.**

Providing QBO Information

To continue QBO requires additional information, such as the industry your company operates, the types or products you sell etc.

To provide QBO additional information (continuing from above), do the following:

1   Type the information provided in Figure 1.3 into the Welcome to QuickBooks window. You will need to replace the Company Name as shown with your name and your identification number as specified by your instructor.

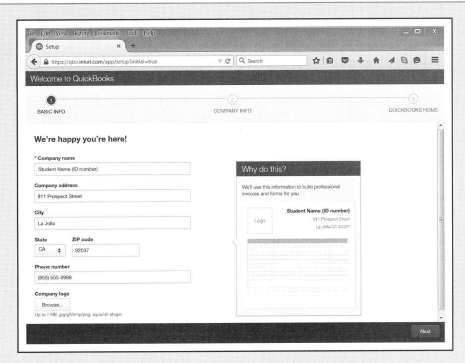

Figure 1.3

Basic Info window

QUICKBOOKS SUPPORT

1-888-859-4056

WWW.QUICKBOOKS.COM/ SUPPORT

2 Click **Next**.

3 Type the information provided in Figure 1.4 into the Welcome to QuickBooks window.

4 Select the appropriate option buttons and check boxes shown in Figure 1.4. The company does not accept wire transfers, ACH.

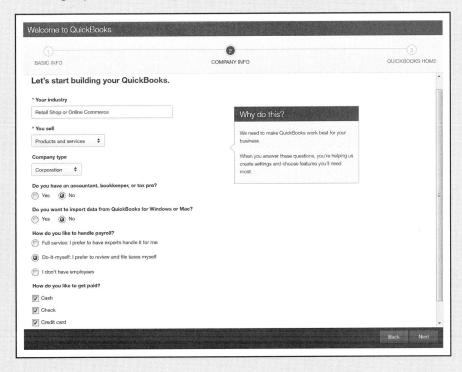

Figure 1.4

Company Info window

5   Click **Next**. After a minute or so, the information in Figure 1.5 appears.

Figure 1.5

Company Info window (QBO customization)

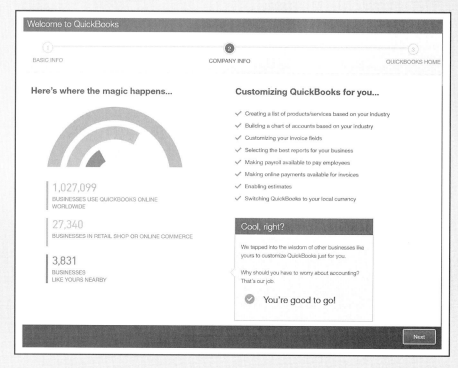

6   Review the information provided, and click **Next** to view the Home page shown in Figure 1.6. Upon entry, the Home page opens the Create (+) menu. More on this later.

Figure 1.6

Create (+) menu

7   Click anywhere outside the Create (+) menu to view the Home page shown in Figure 1.7.

Figure 1.7

Home page

Navigating QBO

The Home page provides links to various tasks and resources. The Customers window provides access to adding new customers, viewing existing balances, and highlighting overdue accounts. The Vendors window provides access to adding new vendors, viewing existing balances, and highlighting overdue accounts. The Employees window provides access to adding new employees and viewing payroll information. To begin, you should review the Welcome Guide, which provides tasks to help you get started. In particular, you want to learn how to navigate around QBO.

To use the Welcome Guide, do the following:

1 Click **Welcome Guide** from Home to open a new tab in your browser shown in Figure 1.8.

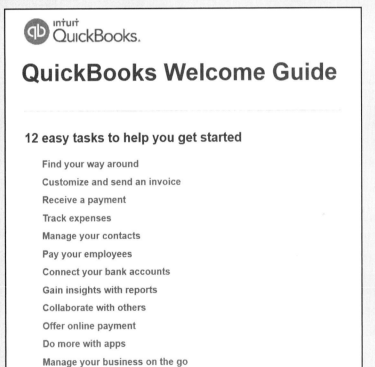

Figure 1.8

QuickBooks Welcome Guide

2 Click **Find your way around** to view Figure 1.9, which illustrates the various parts of the Home page.

Figure 1.9

Find your way around
(QBO Home page details)

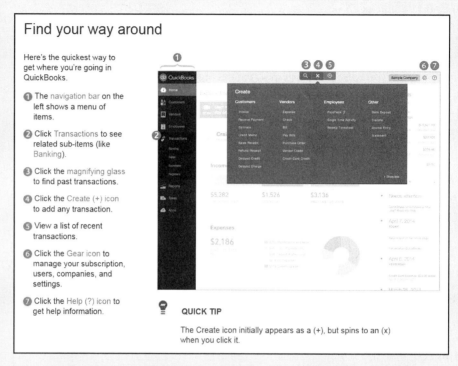

Find your way around

Here's the quickest way to get where you're going in QuickBooks.

❶ The navigation bar on the left shows a menu of items.

❷ Click Transactions to see related sub-items (like Banking).

❸ Click the magnifying glass to find past transactions.

❹ Click the Create (+) icon to add any transaction.

❺ View a list of recent transactions.

❻ Click the Gear icon to manage your subscription, users, companies, and settings.

❼ Click the Help (?) icon to get help information.

QUICK TIP

The Create icon initially appears as a (+), but spins to an (x) when you click it.

3   Close the Welcome Guide and return to the Home page.

4   Click **Customers** from the navigation bar on the left of the Home page to view Figure 1.10. Remember QBO is an online application and Intuit will change it often. Thus the figures in this text may differ from what you see in QBO online.

Figure 1.10

Customers window

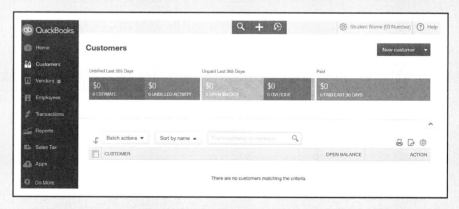

5   Click **Vendors** from the navigation bar on the left of the Home page to view Figure 1.11.

Figure 1.11

Vendors window

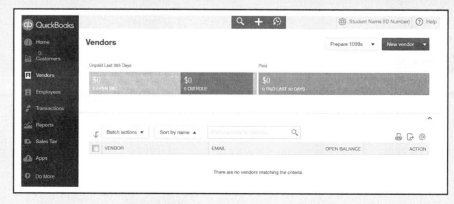

6 Click the **Gear** icon located in the upper right-hand corner of the Home page to Figure 1.12.

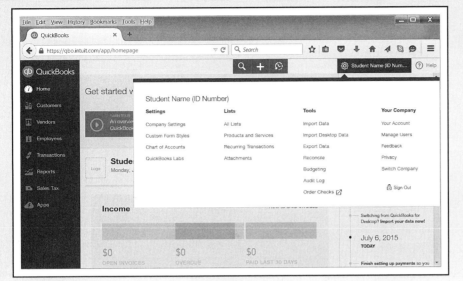

Figure 1.12

Gear window

7 Click **Home** to return to the Home page.

Assigning an Instructor as the Company's "Accountant"

Your instructor may require you to assign him or her as your Company's accountant. You do this so he or she, as your accountant, will always have access to your company files for grading and evaluation purposes. This will also assist the instructor in answering questions you may have about your company. The process of assigning an accountant to your company involves a brief interview in which you will provide your instructor's email address and name. Make sure you have that information before beginning this process. Your instructor will receive an email inviting him or her to be your accountant. Once the instructor accepts your invitation, he or she will have access to your company and the instructor's name will appear in the Accounting Firms section of the Manage Users page.

To assign an accountant to your company, do the following:

1 From the home page, click the **Gear** icon.

2 Click **Manage Users** shown in Figure 1.13.

Figure 1.13

Gear window (Manage Users option)

3   Click **Invite Accountant** shown in Figure 1.14

Figure 1.14

Manage Users window
(inviting instructor as accountant)

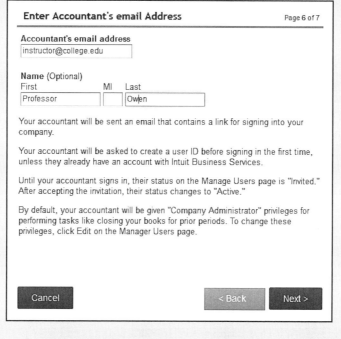

4   Type your instructor's email address and name in the space provided and click **Next** shown in Figure 1.15.

Figure 1.15

Accountant's information
(instructor information to QBO)

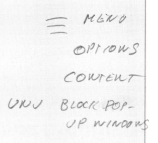

5   Click **Finish**.

Using QBO's Help Feature

QBO provides help with a handy search feature. Help comes in two forms: built-in from Intuit and dynamic help from the QuickBooks Community.

To access Help from within QBO, do the following:

1   Click **Help** located in the upper right of the Home page to access QBO help. (In fact, help is available in all windows.)

2 Type **chart of accounts** in the search box of the Help window to see available help shown in Figure 1.16. *Trouble!* Be quick because if you wait too long, QBO will revert to the Top help topics list.

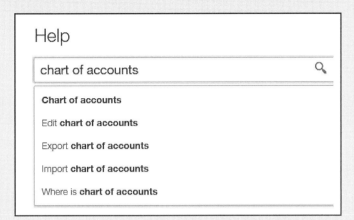

Figure 1.16

Help window (searching chart of accounts)

3 Click the text **Where is the chart of accounts** to view Figure 1.17. *Trouble*! Be quick because if you wait too long, QBO will revert to the Top help topics list. If this happens, retype chart of accounts in the search box.

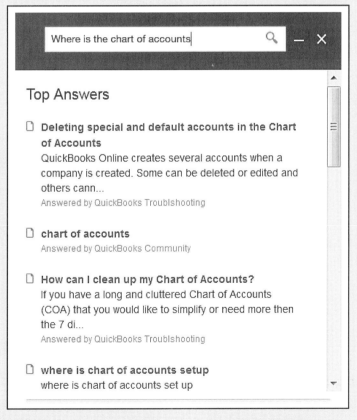

Figure 1.17

Help window (searching chart of accounts location)

4 Scroll down the help window and then click the text **Where is chart of accounts setup** to view a QuickBooks Community response shown in Figure 1.18. Because this is a dynamic help and may change daily, your window may differ.

Figure 1.18

Help window (answer)

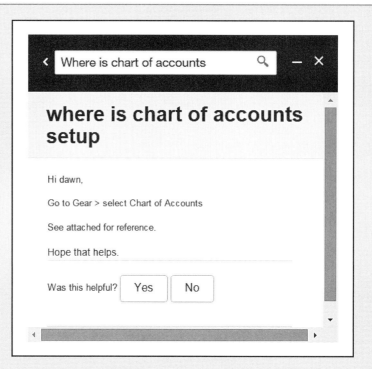

5   Close the Help Answer window.

6   Click the **Gear** icon and click **Sign Out**.

End Note

You have now been introduced to QBO, its basic features, and how it is similar to but not the same as QBDT. You created your Intuit account and provided basic information about your company and learned how to navigate around the QBO application. After assigning your instructor as your accountant and learning more about the help features in QBO, you are ready to learn more about the application by exploring a sample company provided by Intuit in Chapter 2. Don't worry because you will be back to your company in Chapter 3.

Chapter 1 Questions

1 How are QBO and QBDT different in the number of companies they can manage per license?

2 Does QBO work offline, without an Internet connection?

3 Do you need to back up QBO files?

4 How are QBO and QBDT similar?

5 What information do you need to supply to assign your instructor as the company's accountant?

Chapter 1 Matching

a. QBO   _____ Click to access help

b. QBDT   _____ Click to find past transactions

c. Gear icon   _____ Provides tasks to help you get started

d. Welcome Guide   _____ Online version of QuickBooks

e. Navigation bar   _____ Click to add your instructor as your accountant

f. Create (+) icon   _____ Provides links to QBO tasks and resources

g. Magnifying Glass   _____ Windows Desktop version of QuickBooks

h. Help (?) icon   _____ Click to add any transaction

i. Manage Users   _____ Click to manage your subscription, users, and settings

j. Home page   _____ On the left of the Home page, it shows a menu of items

Sample Company Walkthrough

Overview

Intuit has provided a Sample Company online to provide new users a test drive of its QBO product. You will open this Sample Company and explore various features of QBO. In this chapter, you will be viewing the Sample Company looking at customer, vendor, and employee information. You will also be viewing banking, sales, and expense transactions and will be looking at the chart of accounts, lists, reports, and company settings. You will not be making any changes, such as adding a customer, invoice, check, etc. That will occur in the next chapter.

The author has no control over the dates used by Intuit, and those dates may change, depending on when you are accessing the file online. The dates which appear in the figures supplied by the author in this text may not be the dates which appear on your screen.

Begin Your Sample Company Walkthrough

You can use this Sample Company to explore QBO as often as you like. No matter what you do to modify this Sample Company, you will be unable to save it. When you leave and later return, it will look the same as it did initially. Each time you open this Sample Company, it will retrieve your current system date (the actual date you are working on your computer) and place that date under the company name on the home page.

To open the Sample Company, do the following:

1 Open your Internet browser.

2 Type **https://qbo.intuit.com/redir/testdrive** into your browser's address text box, and press [**Enter**] to view the Sample Company Home page shown in Figure 2.1. You may be asked to provide security information before proceeding. If so, type the words provided into the text box and click **Continue**. Your system date will differ from the date shown under the company name in the figure below. Transaction dates may also differ on your screen from the figures shown throughout this text.

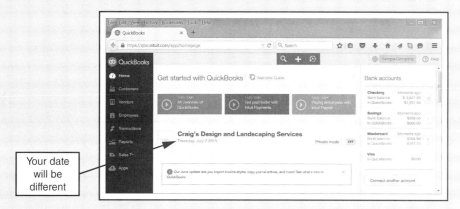

Figure 2.1

Sample Company Home page

In Chapter 1, you used the Welcome Guide to better acquaint you with the Home page. The Find your way around section of the Welcome Guide is shown below in Figure 2.2 as a reminder. As you explore the navigation bar, you will be directed to right-click tasks so they open up in a new tab in your browser. This will facilitate viewing multiple sections of QBO easily.

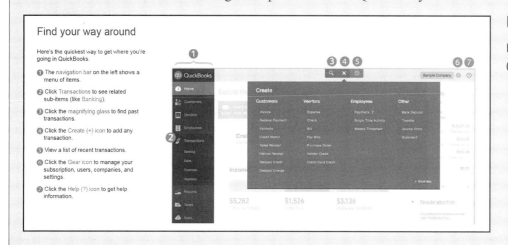

Figure 2.2

Find your way around (Home page overview)

Customers, Vendors, and Employees

QBO provides easy access to customer information using the navigation bar. In this section, you will open the Customers section in a new tab and drill down to a specific customer and specific transactions relate to that customer.

To access customer information, do the following:

1 Right-click **Customers** from the navigation bar and select **Open Link in New Tab** shown in Figure 2.3.

Figure 2.3

Home page (right-click to view Customers in a new tab)

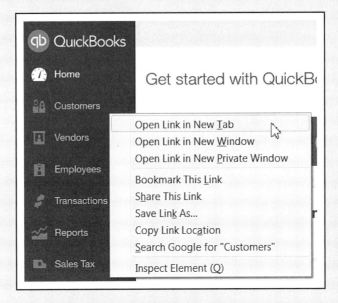

2 Click on the new **Customers tab**. The resulting action will add a new tab to your browser shown in Figure 2.4.

Figure 2.4

Home page (Customers window in a new tab)

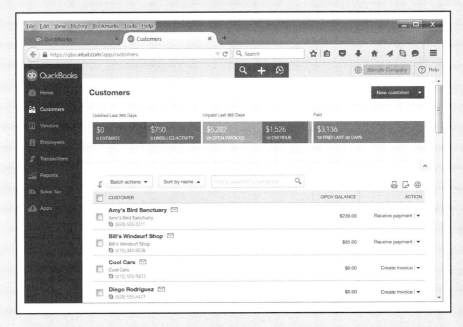

3 Click on the text **Amy's Bird Sanctuary** to view detail transactions related to that particular customer shown in Figure 2.5

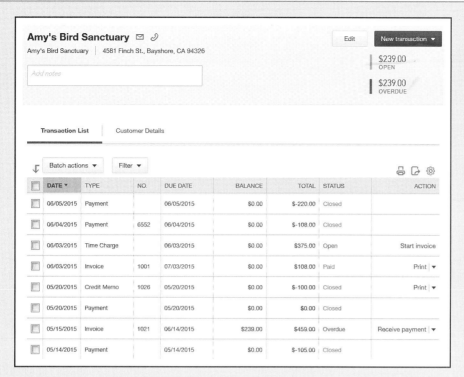

Figure 2.5

Amy's Bird Sanctuary

The $239.00 overdue balance noted at the top of the window correlates to invoice 1021 shown near the bottom of the figure. (The author has no control over the dates used by Intuit, and those dates may change depending on when you are accessing the file online. The dates, which appear in the figures supplied by the author in this text, may not match the dates that appear on your screen.)

QBO provides easy access to vendor information using the navigation bar. In this section, you will open the Vendors section in a new tab and drill down to a specific vendor and specific transactions related to that vendor.

To access vendor information, do the following:

1 Right-click **Vendors** from the navigation bar and select **Open Link in New Tab**. The resulting action will add a new tab to your browser.

2 Click on the new **Vendors** tab to reveal a Vendor listing shown in Figure 2.6.

Figure 2.6

Vendors information

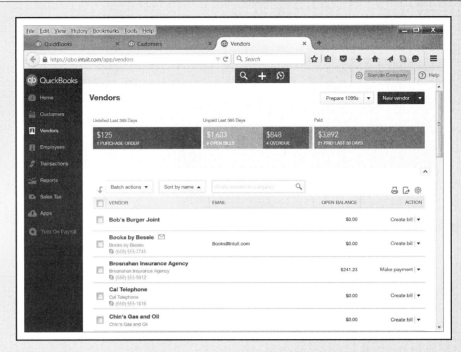

3 Click on the text **Brosnahan Insurance Agency** to view detail transactions related to that particular vendor shown in Figure 2.7

Figure 2.7

Brosnahan Insurance Agency

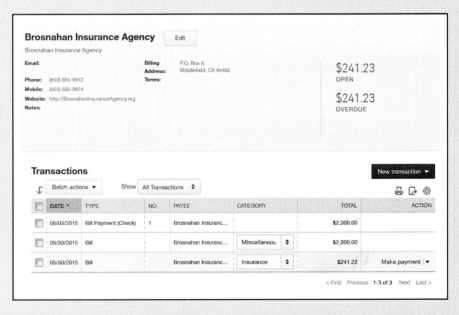

4 Double-click on the **$241.23** balance to view the bill received and shown in Figure 2.8.

Figure 2.8

Bill from Brosnahan Insurance Agency

The $241.23 overdue balance noted at the top of the window correlates to a bill received from an earlier month.

QBO provides easy access to employee information using the navigation bar. In this section, you will open the Employees section in a new tab and drill down to a specific employee and specific transactions related to that employee.

To access employee information, do the following:

1 Right-click **Employees** from the navigation bar and then select **Open Link in New Tab**. The resulting action will add a new tab to your browser.

2 Click on the new **Employees** tab to reveal an Employee listing shown in Figure 2.9.

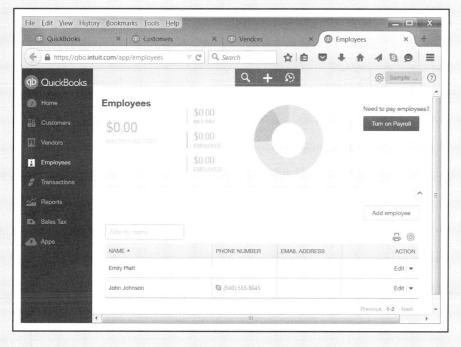

Figure 2.9

Employees information

1   Click on the text **Edit** for John Johnson to view employee information for John Johnson shown in Figure 2.10.

Figure 2.10

Employee information for John Johnson

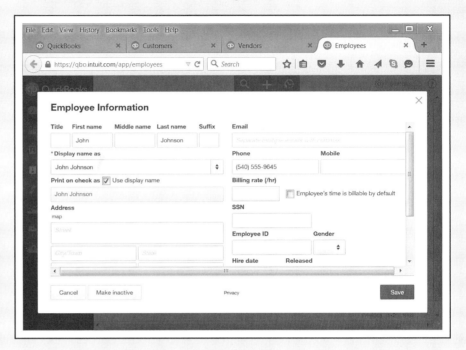

2   Click **Cancel** to close this window.

3   Click the **Gear** icon, and click **Sign Out** to close the Sample Company.

Banking Transactions

QBO has an online banking feature that lets you automatically connect to your bank and download banking-related transactions. The application automatically matches the banking transaction with a previously recorded QBO transaction. QBO calls this "Recognizing". This feature is briefly reviewed since this text is academically based and no "real" bank account is linked to this sample and no "real" bank account will be linked to your student company.

To view banking transactions, do the following:

1   Open your Internet browser.

2   Type **https://qbo.intuit.com/redir/testdrive** into your browser's address text box and then press [**Enter**] to view the Sample Company Home page shown in Figure 2.1. You may be asked to provide security information before proceeding. If so, type the words provided into the text box and then click **Continue**.

3   Click **Transactions** and then click **Banking** from the Navigation Bar on the home page to view the **Bank and Credit Cards** page of the Sample Company.

4   Select **Checking** from the drop-down menu at the top of the window to
     view the window shown in Figure 2.11.

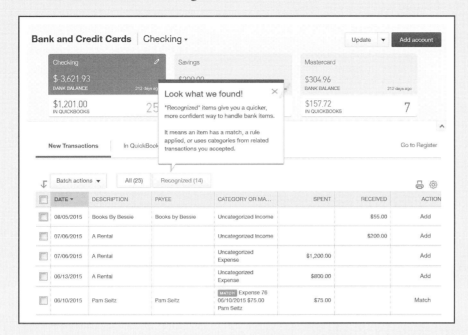

Figure 2.11

Bank and Credit Cards
(partial view)

5   Click the **X** to close the note and click the **Recognized** (14) tab to view
     the listing of only those banking transactions recognized by QBO shown
     in Figure 2.12.

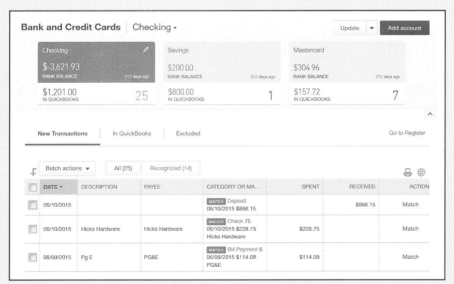

Figure 2.12

Bank and Credit Cards
(recognized banking
transactions: partial view)

6   Click **Go to Register** on the right to view the traditional checking account
     register listing each QBO recorded check, deposit, or cash transaction
     affecting the checking account shown in Figure 2.13 below. Close any
     messages that may appear.

Figure 2.13

Bank Register (partial view)

The "Look What We Found" message in Figure 2.11 indicates that some of the banking transactions matched QBO transactions. Also, the All (25) tab is selected meaning the listing provided represents all banking transactions whether they were recognized or not.

Bank deposits, which have not been recorded in QBO, are not recognized and are temporarily classified as Uncategorized Income. Bank charges that have not been recorded in QBO are not recognized and are temporarily classified as Uncategorized Expense.

The Register seen in Figure 2.13 is similar to the general ledger account concept seen in traditional accounting without the debits and credits. The balance is shown after every increase or decrease in the account. In a bank account, increases are deposits and decreases are payments. Registers exist for all asset, liabilities, and equity accounts and are a great way to identify and/or correct errors if they occur.

Sales and Expense Transactions

The next two choices in the navigation bar are sales and expenses transactions. The sales transaction section will provide a listing of recent sales invoices and payments: Some are closed and others are open, meaning payment has not been received. Thus, the action of receiving payment is listed for all open invoices. This screen also highlights unbilled activity, open balances, overdue balances, and those invoices paid in the last 30 days across the top. You can decide to drill down to view a particular invoice.

To view sales and expenses transactions, do the following:

1   Click **Sales** (located under the Transactions heading) from the navigation bar to view the Sales section shown in Figure 2.14.

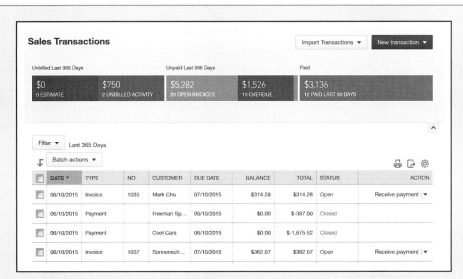

Figure 2.14

Sales Transactions (partial view)

2 Double-click on Invoice No. **1035** to reveal the invoice shown in Figure 2.15.

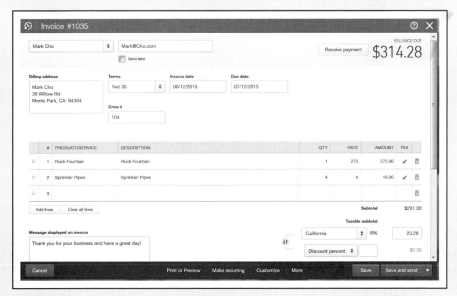

Figure 2.15

Invoice # 1035

3 Click **Cancel** to close Invoice No. 1035.

The expenses section will provide a listing of recent credit card transactions, bills, expenses, purchase orders, checks, bill payments, and cash transactions. You can decide to drill down to view a particular credit card transaction.

4 Click **Expenses** (located under the Transactions heading) from the navigation bar to view the Expense Transactions section shown in Figure 2.16.

Figure 2.16

Expense Transactions
(partial view)

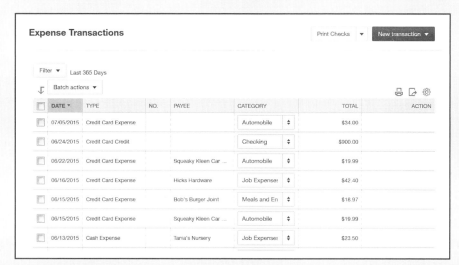

5   Double-click the Credit Card Expense for $19.99 with payee **Squeaky Kleen Car Wash** to reveal the charge shown in Figure 2.17.

Figure 2.17

Expense window (credit card charge for $19.99)

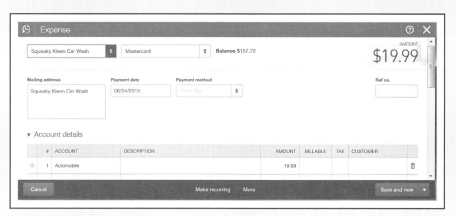

6   Click **Cancel** to close the credit card charge window.

Chart of Accounts

A chart of accounts is a listing of all accounts available. Each account is assigned a type and a detailed type. The Sample Company's chart of accounts has been modified from the default chart of accounts and tailored to this company's needs. Not all companies need these particular accounts, and some will need additional accounts.

To view the Sample Company's chart of accounts, do the following:

1   Click **Chart of Accounts** (located under the Transactions heading) from the navigation bar to view the Chart of Accounts section shown in Figure 2.18.

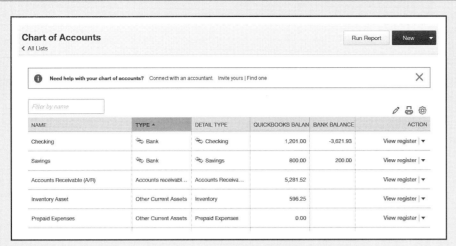

Figure 2.18

Chart of Accounts (partial view)

2 Scroll down the chart of accounts. Each asset, liabilities, and equity account has a View Register action item listed.

3 As you scroll down, you will see that the balance in the chart of accounts for accounts payable (A/P) is $1,602.67.

4 Click **View Register** on the Accounts Payable line of the chart of accounts to view the Register for accounts payable shown in Figure 2.19. The ending balance in the A/P Register matches the $1,602.67 balance specified in the chart of accounts listing. (Remember to ignore dates in this Sample problem.)

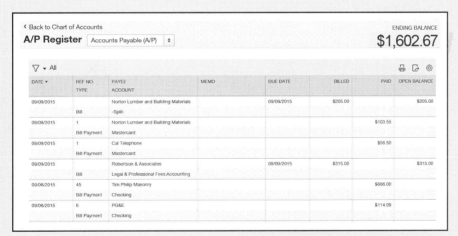

Figure 2.19

A/P Register

5 Click **Back to Chart of Accounts** located at the top of the A/P Register.

6 Scroll down the chart of accounts to see that each revenue and expense account has a Run Report action item listed. Click on **Run Report** on the Landscaping Service account line to view an Account Quickreport for the Landscaping Services account.

7 In the Transaction Date text box, click the drop-down list and select ~~This~~ Year-to-date, then click **Run Report** to view the report shown in Figure 2.20.

LHSI

Figure 2.20

Account Quickreport

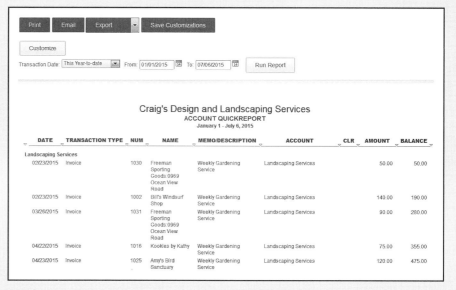

Lists

Lists in QBO provide you with an easy and quick way to view a collection of common items. Some of the more common lists include the chart of accounts, products and services, and terms. You can decide to view a summary of all the lists available in QBO and explore the list of terms.

To view a list of lists and the list of terms, do the following:

8 Click the **Gear** icon and then click **All Lists** to view a list of lists shown in Figure 2.21.

Figure 2.21

Lists

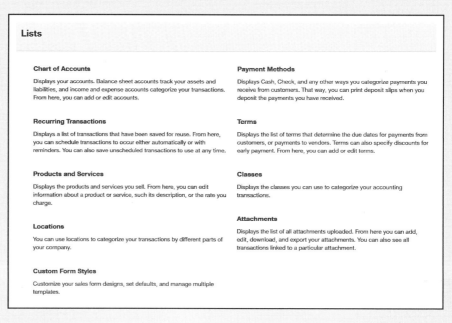

9 Click **Terms** to view the list shown in Figure 2.22.

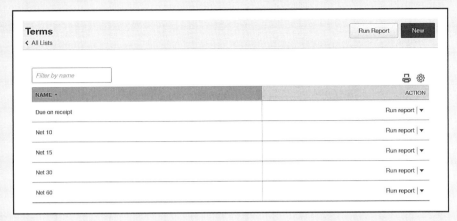

Figure 2.22

Terms

Reports

QBO comes with many predesigned reports for use in business, all of which you can customize for your particular needs. For instance, you can decide to focus on the common financial statement reports: the Income Statement (known in QBO as the Profit and Loss report), Balance sheet, and Statement of Cash Flows.

1 Click **Reports** (located under the Transactions heading) from the navigation bar,

2 Click **All Reports**, and

3 Click **Business Overview**.

4 Scroll down the page to see **Business Overview** report options shown in Figure 2.23.

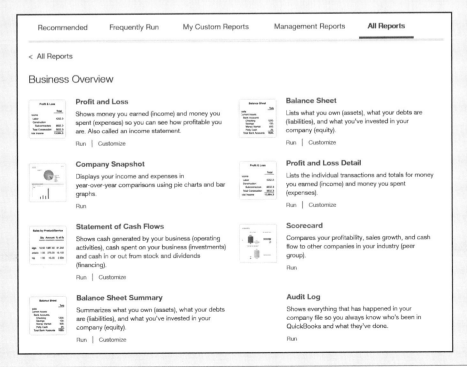

Figure 2.23

Business Overview reports

5 Click **Profit and Loss** and click **Collapse** to view the report shown in Figure 2.24. (You will learn more about customizing and creating other reports in Chapter 10. Remember, the dates on your screen may differ from those shown in the figure.)

Figure 2.24

Profit and Loss report

Craig's Design and Landscaping Services
PROFIT AND LOSS
January 1 - July 8, 2015

	TOTAL
Income	
Design income	2,250.00
Discounts given	-89.50
Landscaping Services	6,513.97
Pest Control Services	110.00
Sales of Product Income	912.75
Services	503.55
Total Income	**$10,200.77**
Cost of Goods Sold	
Cost of Goods Sold	405.00
Total Cost of Goods Sold	**$405.00**
Gross Profit	**$9,795.77**
Expenses	
Advertising	74.86
Automobile	463.37
Equipment Rental	112.00
Insurance	241.23
Job Expenses	957.89
Legal & Professional Fees	1,170.00
Maintenance and Repair	940.00
Meals and Entertainment	28.49
Office Expenses	18.08
Rent or Lease	900.00
Utilities	331.39
Total Expenses	**$5,237.31**
Net Operating Income	**$4,558.46**
Other Expenses	
Miscellaneous	2,916.00
Total Other Expenses	**$2,916.00**
Net Other Income	**$ -2,916.00**
Net Income	**$1,642.46**

6 Click **Reports** and click **Balance Sheet** to view the Balance Sheet report shown in Figure 2.25.

BALANCE SHEET DETAIL

Figure 2.25

Balance Sheet (trimmed to view in one figure)

7   Click **Reports** and click **Statement of Cash Flows** to view the Statement of Cash Flows report shown in Figure 2.26.

Figure 2.26

Statement of Cash Flows

Alternatively, you can easily find a report if you know its name or part of its name. For example, if you wanted to access a report dealing with accounts receivable (A/R), you would type A/R into the report search box located in the Reports section.

To find a report related to accounts receivable, do the following:

8 Click **Reports** and type **A/R** in the Reports search box shown in Figure 2.27.

Figure 2.27

Reports

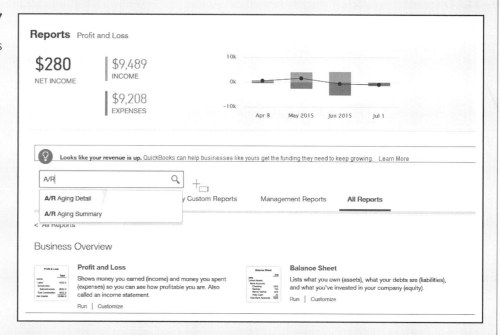

Company Settings

Four tabs are in the Settings section of QBO: Company, Sales, Expenses, and Advanced. You can edit these by clicking on the Pencil icon to the right of each section. The settings for the Sample Company have been modified from the default settings provided when QBO first creates a company. These options in the Settings section change the way QBO appears to the user. For example, in the Advanced section, if time tracking is turned off, no time tracking features will be available in QBO. Also, if purchase orders are turned off in the Expenses section, no purchase orders will be available in QBO. You can decide to view each of these sections to learn more about what options you are given in QBO.

ACCOUNT AND SETTINGS

9 Click the **Gear** icon and then click **Company Settings** and click the **Company** tab to view the company settings section shown in Figure 2.28.

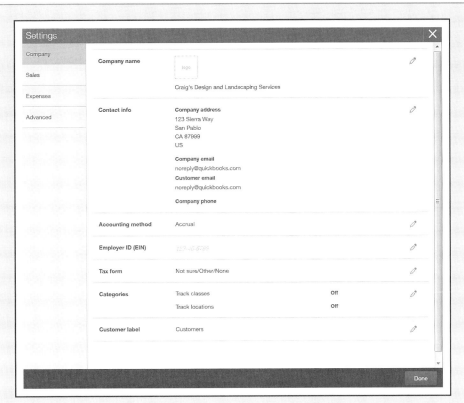

Figure 2.28

Company settings

10 Click the **Sales** tab in the **Settings** window to view options provided shown in Figure 2.29.

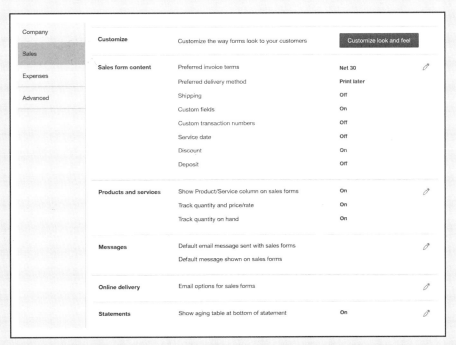

Figure 2.29

Sales settings

11 Click the **Expenses** tab in the **Settings** window to view options provided shown in Figure 2.30.

Figure 2.30

Expenses settings

12   Click the **Advanced** tab in the **Settings** window to view options provided shown in Figure 2.31.

Figure 2.31

Advanced settings

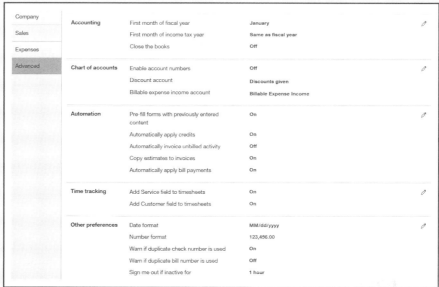

13   Click **Done** to close the **Settings** window.

End Note

In this chapter, you have used Intuit's Sample Company to practice navigating QBO. You have accessed customer, vendor, and employee information, viewed various transactions, and viewed the chart of accounts, lists, reports, and company settings. In Chapters 4 through 10, you will use the same Sample Company to learn how to add operating, investing, and financing activities, reconcile a bank account, create a budget, add adjusting entries, and prepare financial statements and reports. In Chapter 3, you will return to your company and modify default settings, add new accounts and beginning balances, and add customers, vendors, products, and services.

Chapter 2 Questions

1 What steps do you take to view customer information in a new tab?

2 What steps do you take to view detail transactions related to a particular customer?

3 What steps do you take to view a specific bill from a specific vendor?

4 What steps do you take to view a specific employee's information?

5 How are bank deposits, which have not been recorded in QBO, classified?

6 How are bank charges, which have not been recorded in QBO, classified?

7 Opening the sales transaction section of QBO will provide a listing of _____.

8 Opening the expense transaction section of QBO will provide a listing of _____.

9 What lists are available in QBO?

10 What steps do you take to view all reports related to accounts payable (A/P)?

Chapter 2 Matching

a. Navigation bar

b. Amy's Bird Sanctuary

c. Brosnahan Insurance Agency

d. Recognizing

e. Uncategorized Income

f. Uncategorized Expense

g. Registers

h. John Johnson

i. Terms

j. Chart of accounts

_____ An employee in the Sample Company

_____ Bank deposits not yet recognized

_____ Exist for all asset, liability, and equity accounts

_____ Specify due dates for payment to/from vendors/customers

_____ Used to access a list of sales and expense transactions

_____ A vendor in the Sample Company

_____ A listing of all accounts available

_____ Bank charges not yet recognized

_____ A customer in the Sample Company

_____ Matching a banking transaction with a QBO transaction

Setting Up a New Company

Upon completion of this chapter, the student will be able to do the following:

- Log into their account
- Change company settings
- Modify the chart of accounts, establish beginning balances, and create new customers, vendors, products, and services
- Close opening balance equity and create a trial balance
- Create, print, and export a transaction detail by account report

Overview

You began this process in Chapter 1 when you created your account and provided basic information about your company including the company name, address, industry, type, etc. Now it's time to continue that process.

First off, however, you're going to revisit the sample company you worked on in Chapter 2. Each of the following chapters will work the same way. To begin, you will navigate your browser to the Intuit Sample Company. The text will demonstrate how to do certain tasks, such as modify defaults, add a new account, add a new transaction etc. These demonstrations will occur in the Sample Company. Remember, you can modify the Sample Company throughout each session but once you close your browser window, QBO will not remember any of your activity in the Sample Company. When you navigate your browser back to the sample company, it will appear as it first did.

Each section of every chapter will begin with a demonstration using the Sample Company. That is followed by you logging back into QBO with the user name and password you created in Chapter 1 to complete an end of chapter case. In the case, you will be asked to perform tasks similar to those demonstrated in the Sample Company but now in your company. The tasks you accomplish on your company, named Student Name (ID Number), are permanent and will be there after you close your QBO browser window. There is no Save File or Save File As command in QBO. Everything is saved for you.

Company Settings

You can use this Sample Company to explore QBO as often as you would like. No matter what you do to modify this Sample Company, you will not be able to save it. When you leave and later return, it will look the same as it did initially.

To modify Sample Company settings, do the following:

1 Open your Internet browser.

2 Type **https://qbo.intuit.com/redir/testdrive** into your browser's address text box, and press [**Enter**] to view the Sample Company Home page. The system may ask you to provide security information before proceeding. If so, type the words provided into the text box, and click **Continue**.

3 From the Sample Company home page, click the **Gear** icon next to the Sample Company name to manage your settings shown in Figure 3.1.

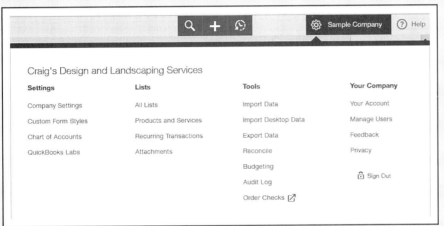

Figure 3.1

Settings

ACCOUNTS AND SETTINGS

4 Click ~~Company Settings~~. The first screen shown is the Sample Company default information shown in Figure 3.2.

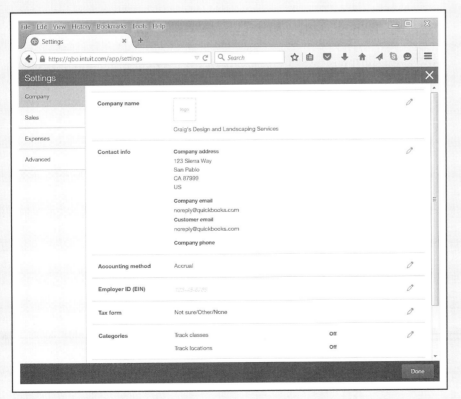

Figure 3.2

Company settings

When you modify the settings of your company, you will visit this section of QBO to make changes and start by selecting the Pencil icon to edit each individual section. You reviewed the four sections of the Company Settings window: Company, Sales, Expenses, and Advanced in Chapter 2. The most common changes to Company Settings involve turning on inventory, tracking of quantities on hand, tracking expenses by customer, making expenses and items billable, establishing default bill payment terms, using purchase orders, and time tracking.

Once you have modified the company settings, it is time to modify the chart of accounts.

Modify the Chart of Accounts and Establish Beginning Balances

You will continue your use of the Sample Company to learn the process of creating, modifying, and deleting accounts and of establishing beginning balances. If you are continuing from above, you will not need to open the Sample Company again. If not, follow the steps above to view the Sample Company. You should complete this entire section in one sitting so you do not lose your work. If you do leave and return, the cumulative balances will be inaccurate as your work will not have been saved while working in the Sample Problem.

Creating accounts and related beginning balances only occurs when you are utilizing QBO for the first time and your business has been in operation for some time. The transition to QBO from a previous accounting system will indicate business events and balances occurred prior to the first date of QBO use.

In this section, you will be adding new checking, inventory, prepaid rent, long-term debt, and common stock accounts to the Sample Company. You will also be establishing beginning balances for checking, accounts receivable, prepaid rent, inventory, and accounts payable. Every time you add a beginning balance, an equal and opposite amount is recorded to the Opening Balance Equity account (to keep debits and credits in balance).

QBO lets you establish a beginning amount for all of these accounts using basic journal entries. We will do that for some accounts, accounts receivable, accounts payable, and common stock. For the other accounts, such as checking, inventory, prepaid rent, long-term debt, and common stock, you will set some beginning balances when you set up a new account.

When a new account is added its category type needs to be specified. Asset category types include the following: bank, accounts receivable, other current assets, fixed assets, and other assets. Liability category types include the following: accounts payable, credit cards, other current liabilities, and long-term liabilities. Equity is its own category type. Revenue category types include income and other income. Expense category types include cost of goods sold, expenses, and other expense. Every account needs to be assigned to one of these category types. This will dictate where the account appears in all reports, especially the income statement, balance sheet, and statement of cash flows. The detailed category type will further define where the account appears under its category type. Examples of bank category detailed types include cash on hand, checking, money market, and savings.

To begin, let's add a new checking account with a beginning balance of $20,000.00.

To add a new checking account to the chart of accounts and establish a beginning balance, do the following:

1 Click **Transactions** and click **Chart of Accounts** from the Navigation bar.

← BACK 1 PAGE

2 View the chart of accounts. Only one checking account has a Quick-Books balance of $1,201.00.

BACK TO CHART OF ACCOUNTS

3 Click the **New** button in the upper right-hand corner of the chart of accounts.

4 Click anywhere in the **Category Type** text box and select **Bank** shown in Figure 3.3.

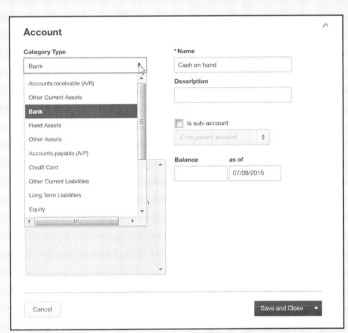

Figure 3.3

Account (adding a new bank account)

5 Select **Checking** from the Detail Type list and type **Checking BOA** in the **Name** text box.

6 Type **20000** in the Balance text box and type ~~12/31/14~~ in the as of text box shown in Figure 3.4.   *01/31/2017*

Figure 3.4

Account (completing the addition
of a new checking account)

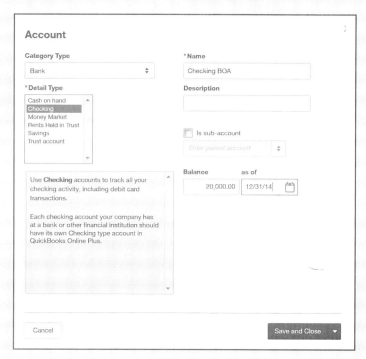

7   Click the **Save and Close** button to view the modified chart of accounts
    shown in Figure 3.5, which now includes a new checking account with a
    balance of $20,000.00.

Figure 3.5

Chart of Accounts (modified with
the new checking BOA account)

01 / 1 / 2017

So far, we have added a $20,000 increase to the assets to the Sample Com-
pany as of ~~12/31/14~~. The Opening Balance Equity account has also increased as
the result of this adjustment. To continue, let's add a new product. In QBO,
products are merchandise a company purchases from a vendor, maintains in inventory, and then sells to customers. Services are efforts made by a company to
add value to a customer. In the Sample Company, an inventory account exists.
If you create a new company, an inventory account may not exist. However,
when you add a new product, a new inventory account, called inventory asset,
will automatically be created.

To add a new product and service, do the following:

1   View the chart of accounts and note the Inventory Asset account with
    a QuickBooks balance of $596.25.

2   Click the **Gear** icon and click **Products and Services** from the Lists column.

3   Click **New**.

4   Select **Item** from the ~~Select a Product Type~~ drop down list.   *INVENTORY*

5   Type **Stone Tile** as the new product Name text box.

6   Place a check in the "**I track quantity. . .**" check box.   *NOT THERE*

7   Type **500** in the Initial Quantity on Hand text box and ~~12/31/2014~~ in   *01/31/2017*
the **As Of Date** text box.

8   Leave **Inventory Asset** as the Inventory Asset Account.   *↓ SCROLL DOWN*

9   Type **Stone Tile** as the description for the sales and purchase forms.

10   Type **2.50** as the Price and **1.25** as the Cost.

11   Select **Sales of Product Income** as the Income Account and **Cost of Goods Sold** as the Expense Account.

12   Check the **Is taxable** check box. Your window should look like Figure 3.6.

Figure 3.6

Product or Service Information (adding a new product)

13   Click the down-arrow in the Save and Close button and then select **Save and New**.

14   Select **Service** from the **Select a Product Type** drop down list.

15   Type **Estimates** as the name of a new service.

16   Check the **I sell this product/service to my customers** check box.

17   Type **Estimates** as the description.

18   Type **50** as the Price/Rate.

19   Uncheck the **Is taxable** checkbox.

20   Click the **Save and Close** button.

21   Scroll down the list of products and services. Note the addition of the new Stone Tile product, with a quantity of 500, and the new Estimates service added.

22   Click **Transactions** and then **Chart of Accounts** from the Navigation Bar and note the new balance in the Inventory Asset account of $1,221.25, which equals the previous balance of 596.25 plus the addition of $625.00 (500 units @ $1.25).

So far, we have added a $20,625 (20,000.00 + 625.00) net increase to the assets to the Sample Company as of 12/31/14. The Opening Balance Equity account has increased as the result of this adjustment. To continue, let's add prepaid rent, long-term debt, and common stock accounts.

To add additional accounts, do the following:

1   Click the **New** button in the upper right-hand corner of the chart of accounts.

2   Click anywhere in the **Category Type** text box, and select **Other Current Assets.**

3   Select **Prepaid Expenses** as the Detail Type, and type **Prepaid Rent** as the name.

4   Type **4000** in the Balance text box and ~~12/31/2014~~ *01/31/2012* in the **As Of Date** text box.

5   Click the down-arrow in the Save and Close button, and select **Save and New**.

6   Click anywhere in the **Category Type** text box, and select **Long Term Liabilities.**

7   Select **Notes Payable** as the Detail Type, and type **Notes Payable Chase** as the name.

8   Type **9000** in the Balance text box and **12/31/2014** in the **As Of Date** text box.

9   Click the down-arrow in the Save and Close button, and select **Save and New**.

10 Click anywhere in the **Category Type** text box, and select **Equity.**

11 Select **Common Stock** as the Detail Type, and type **Common Stock** as the name.

12 Type **1000** in the Balance text box and ~~12/31/2014~~ *01/31/2017* in the **As of Date** text box.

13 Click the down-arrow in the Save and New button, and select **Save and Close**.

14 Scroll down the chart of accounts. Note the addition of the new Prepaid Rent account with a balance of $4,000.00.

15 Continue scrolling down the chart of accounts. Note the addition of the new Notes Payable Chase account with a balance of $9,000.00.

16 Continue scrolling down the chart of accounts. Note the addition of the new Common Stock account with a balance of $1,000.00.

SCROLL DOWN

So far, we have added a $14,625 (20,000 + 625.00 + 4,000.00 − 9,000.00 − 1,000.00) net increase to the assets to the Sample Company as of 12/31/14. The Opening Balance Equity account is also increased as the result of this adjustment.

Lastly, we will set up beginning balances in accounts receivable and accounts payable by using journal entries and add a new customer and vendor at the same time. Journal entries are commonly used to adjust accounts. A customer is an entity to whom you sell products or provide a service. A vendor is an entity from whom you purchase products or services from.

To journalize accounts receivable and payable beginning balances, do the following:

1   Before you leave the chart of accounts, note the Opening Balance Equity account that has a balance of $5,287.50.

    − 14,712.50

2   Click the **Create (+)** icon, and click on **Journal Entry** from the Other column.

    ⊕ UPPER RIGHT

3   Type ~~12/31/2014~~ *01/31/2017* in the **Journal date** text box.

4   Click in the **Account** column and then click the drop-down arrow.

5   Select **Accounts Receivable (A/R)** as the first account, and type **775** in the Debits column.

6   Click in the **Name** column, click the drop-down arrow, and select **+ Add New** to add a new customer related to this balance shown in Figure 3.7.

Figure 3.7

Accounts Receivable and Payable (journalizing beginning balances)

7   Type **Refugio** as the new customer shown in Figure 3.8.

Figure 3.8

New Name (adding a new
customer name)

8   Click **Save** in the New Name box.

9   Select **Accounts Payable (A/P)** as the second account, and type **500** in
     the Credits column.

10   Click in the **Name** column, click the drop-down arrow, and select +
     Add New to add a new vendor.

11   Type **Rockster** as the Name, change the Type to **Vendor,** and click
     Save.

12   Select **Opening Balance Equity** as the Account on line 3, and accept
     275.00 in the credit column. Your journal entry should look like
     Figure 3.9.

Figure 3.9

Journal Entry to Set Up
A/R and A/P

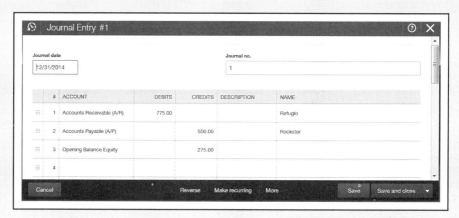

13   Click **Save and Close** to save your work.

14   Scroll down the chart of accounts, and note the Opening Balance
     Equity account, which now has a balance of $5,562.50 (5,287.50 +
     775.00. − 500.00).

9-14,437.50

So far, we have added a $14,900 (20,000 + 625.00 + 4,000.00 − 9,000.00 −
1,000.00 + 775.00 − 500.00) net increase to the assets to the Sample Company
as of 12/31/14. The Opening Balance Equity account has increased as the result
of this adjustment.

Close Opening Balance Equity and Create a Trial Balance

The final step in establishing beginning balances in QBO is to close out the Opening Balance Equity account as of 12/31/14 of $14,900.00. Since we established a common stock account, the only account left in a corporation's equity accounts is retained earnings. Retained earnings is the earnings generated from prior years less dividends. You will need to create a trial balance, which lists the debit or credit balance in all accounts as of a specific date. Your instructor may ask you to customize, print, or export the trial balance to Excel, so you may do that as well.

To close opening balance equity, and create, customize, save, print, and export a trial balance, do the following:

1 Click the **Create (+)** icon, and click on **Journal Entry** from the Other column.

2 Type ~~12/31/2014~~ *01/31/17* in the **Journal date** text box.

3 Select **Opening Balance Equity** as the first account, and type **14900** in the Debits column.

4 Select **Retained Earnings** as the second account, and type **14900** in the Credits column. Your journal entry should look like Figure 3.10.

Figure 3.10

Journal Entry #2 (for closing Opening Balance Equity)

5 Click **Save and close**.

6 Click **Reports** in the Navigation Bar.

7 Type **Trial Balance** into the Go to report search text box, and press [**Enter**].

8 Select **Custom** drop-down list in the Transaction Date text box. *THIS MONTH TO DATE*

9 Type ~~12/31/14~~ in the **From** text box, and press [**Tab**]. *01/01/2017*

10 Type **12/31/14** in the **To** text box, and press [**Tab**].

11 Click the **Run Report** button to view the trial balance shown in Figure 3.11.

Figure 3.11

Trial Balance (as of 12/31/14)

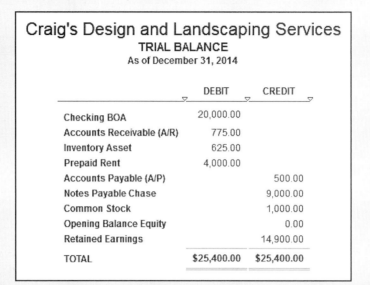

60,418.59   60,418.59

12 Click the **Save Customizations** button.

13 Change the name of the custom report to **Trial Balance 12/31/14**, and place a check in the **Share this report with all company users** check box as shown in Figure 3.12.

Figure 3.12

Save Report Customizations

SHARE WITH ALL

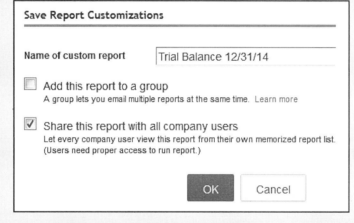

14 Click ~~OK.~~ SAVE

15 Click the **Print** button, and click **OK** to print this report.

16 Click **Close** to close the print window.

17 Click **Export**, and click **Export (XLSX)** to begin the export to Excel process.

18 Type **Trial Balance** as the file name in the Save As window and then click **Save** after you have navigated to a place on your computer to save this file.

19 Open Excel and then open the file you just saved.

20 After viewing your newly created Excel file, close Excel.

E-MAIL TO JSTOKES@robert MORRIS .EDU

CHANGE REGARDS TO NAME

In the Sample Company, other business events occurred after 12/31/14, so the current balance in the Opening Balance Equity account is not zero. You will need to create a Transactions Report to view the underlying transactions in the Opening Balance Equity account from the Trial Balance report. That report will provide details of all transactions for a particular account for a specified period.

To view the activity in this account through 12/31/14, do the following:

1   Click the **0.00** balance in the Opening Balance Equity line of the Trial Balance report shown in Figure 3.11 to view the Transaction Report shown in Figure 3.13.

− 8,712.50

Figure 3.13

Transaction Report (for the Opening Balance Equity Account)

Craig's Design and Landscaping Services
TRANSACTION REPORT
December 31, 2014

DATE	TRANSACTION TYPE	NUM	NAME	MEMO/DESCRIPTION	ACCOUNT	SPLIT	AMOUNT	BALANCE
Opening Balance Equity								
12/31/2014	Journal Entry			Opening Balance	Opening Balance Equity	-Split-	-9,000.00	-9,000.00
12/31/2014	Journal Entry			Opening Balance	Opening Balance Equity	-Split-	-1,000.00	-10,000.00
12/31/2014	Journal Entry	1			Opening Balance Equity	-Split-	275.00	-9,725.00
12/31/2014	Deposit				Opening Balance Equity	Prepaid Rent	4,000.00	-5,725.00
12/31/2014	Deposit				Opening Balance Equity	Checking BOA	20,000.00	14,275.00
12/31/2014	Inventory Qty Adjust	START		Opening inventory for Stone Tile	Opening Balance Equity	Opening Balance Equity	625.00	14,900.00
12/31/2014	Inventory Qty Adjust	START		Opening inventory for Stone Tile	Opening Balance Equity	Inventory Asset		14,900.00
12/31/2014	Journal Entry	2			Opening Balance Equity	-Split-	-14,900.00	0.00
Total for Opening Balance Equity							$0.00	
TOTAL							$0.00	

2   Click the **Save Customizations** button.

3   Type **Transaction Report for Opening Bal Equity** in the **Name of custom report** text box.

4   Click in the **Share this report** check box.   *SAVE?*

5   Click ~~OK.~~ *ALL*

6   Click the **Gear** icon, and click **Sign Out** to sign out of the Sample Company.

Create, Print, and Export a Transaction Detail by Account

Often, you will want to investigate a detail list of transactions you have recorded for a specific period. In your end of chapter cases, a usual explanation for an incorrect report is recording a transaction in the incorrect period. To explore this option, you will create a transaction detail by account report for a specific period. You can create such a report for a large period to see if your transactions were recorded in the proper period and to see where you may have entered a wrong amount or account.

To create, print, and export a transaction detail by account report for the period 1/1/2010 to 12/31/2020, do the following:

1   Open your Internet browser.

2   Type **https://qbo.intuit.com/redir/testdrive** into your browser's address text box and the press [**Enter**] to view the Sample Company Home page. All of your transactions from the Sample Company that you recorded in this chapter are gone since you signed out above. That's okay.

3   Click **Reports** from the Navigation bar.

4   Type **Transaction** in the Go to Report text box.

5   Select **Transaction Detail by Account**.

THIS MONTH TO DATE

6   Select **Custom** from the **Transaction Date** drop-down text box.

7   Type **1/1/2010** in the **From** text box.

8   Type **12/31/2020** in the **To** text box.

9   Click **Run Report**. The top of the report is shown in Figure 3.14.

Figure 3.14

Transaction Detail by Account report (top section)

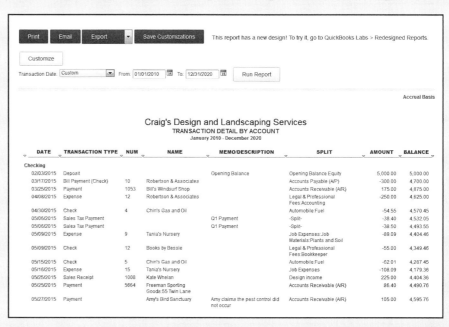

10   Click on **10** to view the Bill Payment (check) written to Robertson & Associates.

11   Close this window, scroll down the report, and investigate other transactions.

12   Scroll back to the top of this report, and click **Save Customizations**.

13   Place a check in the ~~Share this report with all company users~~ check box, and click ~~OK.~~   *ALL*   *SAVE*

NO **14**   ~~Click the~~ **Print** button to set this report up for printing; however, do not print this report since it is too long and unnecessary. Click **Cancel**.

15   Click the **Gear** icon and then click **Sign Out**.

End Note

In this chapter, you have logged into your account with QBO, modified company settings, added new accounts to the chart of accounts and added beginning balances where appropriate. You have added customers, vendors, products and services, closed the Opening Balance Equity account and prepared a trial balance. You are ready to add operating activities like sales receipts, invoices, and cash receipts.

Chapter 3 Questions

1 How do you access Company Settings?

2 When is it appropriate to add beginning balances to accounts?

3 What steps need to be followed to add an account to the chart of accounts?

4 When you add a beginning balance to an account, what other account is affected?

5 What information is required when adding a new product to QBO?

6 What additional information is required when you add beginning balance amounts to the accounts receivable account?

7 What additional information is required when you add beginning balance amounts to the accounts payable account?

8 Which additional account is used when you close Opening Balance Equity?

9 How do you access the Trial Balance report?

10 How can you review a Transactions Report for the Opening Balance Equity account when you are viewing the Trial Balance?

Chapter 3 Matching

a. Transactions report   _____ Entity to whom you sell products/services

b. Trial balance   _____ Account used to offset beginning balances adjustments

c. Journal entry   _____ Merchandise a company purchases from a vendor

d. Opening Balance Equity   _____ Efforts made by a company to add value to a customer

e. Customer   _____ A listing the debit or credit balances as of a specific date

f. Vendor   _____ Dictates where an account appears in all reports

g. Product   _____ Transactions for an account for a specified period

h. Service   _____ Entity from whom you purchase products/services

i. Category Type   _____ Checking

j. Detailed type example   _____ Commonly used to adjust accounts

Chapter 3 Cases

The following cases require you to open the company you created in Chapter 1. Each case below continues throughout the text in a sequential manner. For example, if you are assigned Case 1, you will use the file you modified in this chapter in all following chapters. Each case below is similar in concepts assessed but differs in amounts and transactions.

To reopen your company, do the following:

1 Open your Internet browser.

2 Type **https://qbo.intuit.com/qbo28/login?webredir** into your browser's address text box.

3 Type your User ID and Password into the text boxes as shown in Figure 3.15.

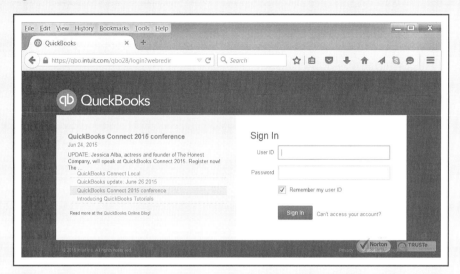

Figure 3.15

Sign In Window (for logging in)

Case 1

Your company is a distributor of surfboards located in La Jolla, California. The company does not collect sales tax since all of its customers are resellers. They began business in 2017 and want to use QBO starting January 1, 2018. Beginning balances as of 12/31/2017 have been provided below.

You must make changes to your company. Many settings are set by default. Do not change any settings unless instructed below. Based on what you learned in the text and using the Sample Company, you are to make the following changes:

1 Modify settings as follows:

a. Company – Company name – Click the Pencil icon to modify the company name to Case 1 – Student Name (ID Number) replacing Student Name with your name and ID Number with the number your instructor indicated.

b. Sales – Turn on – Track quantity on hand. (This will automatically show items table on expense and purchase forms.)

c. Expenses –

   i) Turn on – Track expenses and items by customer
   ii) Turn on – Make expenses and items billable (no markup, track billable expenses and items as income in a single account, no sales tax charged)

iii) Default bill payment terms net 30.

iv) Turn on – Use purchase orders (no custom fields)

d. Payments – no changes

e. Advanced

   i) Time tracking

      (1) Turn on – Add Service field to timesheets

      (2) Turn on – Add Customer field to timesheets

2 Create new accounts and related beginning balances as follows:

Category Type	Detail Type	Name	Balance	As of
Bank	Checking	Checking	25,000.00	12/31/17
Fixed Assets*	Furniture & Fixtures	Original cost	40,000.00	12/31/17
Fixed Assets*	Furniture & Fixtures	Depreciation	10,000.00	12/31/17
Long Term Liabilities	Notes Payable	Notes Payable	60,000.00	12/31/17
Equity	Common Stock	Common Stock	1,000.00	12/31/17

*When entering a new fixed asset place a check in the **Track depreciation of this asset** checkbox to reveal Original cost and Depreciation text boxes. Enter amounts from above as positive numbers.

3 Create two new products and one new service item as follows:

a. Products –

   i) Name/Description – Rook 15, track quantity, initial quantity 12/31/17 – 10, inventory asset account – Inventory Asset (this account will automatically be created in the chart of accounts when you add this product), price - $650, cost – $400, income account – Sales, expense account – Cost of Goods Sold.

   ii) Name/Description – The Water Hog, track quantity, initial quantity 12/31/17 - 8, inventory asset account – Inventory Asset, price – $860, cost – $500, income account – Sales, expense account – Cost of Goods Sold.

b. Service – Name/Description – Consulting, rate - $25, income account – Services.

c. Make changes to the following accounts via journal entry 1 as of 12/31/17 with an offset to Opening Balance Equity:

Account	Amount	Name
Accounts Receivable	5,000.00	Blondie's Boards (new customer)
Prepaid Expenses	3,000.00	
Accounts Payable	4,500.00	Channel Islands (new vendor)

4 Close the Opening Balance Equity account to Retained Earnings via journal entry 2 as of 12/31/17.

5 Prepare and print a Trial Balance report as of 12/31/17, save it as a customized report named Trial Balance 12/31/17, and share it with all users. Your report should look like Figure 3.16.

6 If your trial balance differs from what is in Figure 3.16, do the following:

Figure 3.16

Trial Balance (as of 12/31/17)

Case 1
TRIAL BALANCE
As of December 31, 2017

	DEBIT	CREDIT
Checking	25,000.00	
Accounts Receivable	5,000.00	
Inventory Asset	8,000.00	
Prepaid Expenses	3,000.00	
Furniture & Fixtures:Depreciation		10,000.00
Furniture & Fixtures:Original cost	40,000.00	
Accounts Payable		4,500.00
Notes Payable		60,000.00
Common Stock		1,000.00
Opening Balance Equity		0.00
Retained Earnings		5,500.00
TOTAL	$81,000.00	$81,000.00

    a.   Make sure all of your changes were dated 12/31/17.

    b.   Click on the debit or credit balance to view a transactions report for each account, and investigate why your answer is different.

    c.   Ask you instructor for assistance.

    d.   Be sure your company matches the above since, in the following chapter, you will be adding additional business events.

7   Export your Trial Balance report to Excel, and save it with the file name: Student Name (replace with your name) Ch 03 Case 01 Trial Balance.xlsx.

8   Prepare and print a Transaction Detail by Account report for transactions between 1/1/2010 and 12/31/2020, save it as a customized report named Transaction Detail by Account, and share it with all users. If asked, indicate that your business is accrual based.

9   Use your Transaction Detail by Account report to locate any differences in your Trial Balance report created above.

    a.   Make sure that all of your changes were dated 12/31/17.

    b.   Click on the line that does not match to view the transaction for that account, and investigate why your answer differs.

    c.   Ask you instructor for assistance.

    d.   Be sure your company matches the above since, in the following chapter, you will be adding additional business events.

10   Export your Transactions Detail by Account report to Excel, and save it with the file name: Student Name (replace with your name) Ch 03 Case 01 Transaction Detail by Account.xlsx.

11   Sign out of your company.

Case 2

Your company is a distributor of remote control toys located in La Jolla, California. The company does not collect sales tax since all of its customers are resellers. They began business in 2018 and want to use QBO starting January 1, 2019. Beginning balances as of 12/31/2018 have been provided below.

You must make changes to your company. Based on what you learned in the text and using the Sample Company, you are to make the following changes:

1 Modify settings as follows:

    a. Company – Company name – Click the Pencil icon to modify the company name to Case 2 – Student Name (ID Number) replacing Student Name with your name and ID Number with the number your instructor indicated.

    b. Sales – Turn on – Track quantity on hand. (This will automatically show items table on expense and purchase forms.)

    c. Expenses –

        i) Turn on – Track expenses and items by customer

        ii) Turn on – Make expenses and items billable (no markup, track billable expenses and items as income in a single account, no sales tax charged)

        iii) Default bill payment terms net 30.

        iv) Turn on – Use purchase orders (no custom fields)

    d. Payments – no changes

    e. Advanced

        i) Time tracking

            (1) Turn on – Add Service field to timesheets

            (2) Turn on – Add Customer field to timesheets

2 Create new accounts and related beginning balances as follows:

Category Type	Detail Type	Name	Balance	As of
Bank	Checking	Checking	5,000.00	12/31/18
Fixed Assets*	Machinery & Equipment	Original cost	10,000.00	12/31/18
Fixed Assets*	Machinery & Equipment	Depreciation	1,000.00	12/31/18
Long Term Liabilities	Notes Payable	Notes Payable	12,000.00	12/31/18
Equity	Common Stock	Common Stock	100.00	12/31/18

*When entering a new fixed asset place a check in the **Track depreciation of this asset** checkbox to reveal Original cost and Depreciation text boxes. Enter amounts from above as positive numbers.

3 Create two new products and one new service item:

    a. Products –

        i) Name/Description – Broon F830 Ride, track quantity, initial quantity 12/31/18 – 4, inventory asset account – Inventory Asset (note: this account will automatically be created in the chart of accounts when you add this product), price – $1,500, cost – $800, income account – Sales, expense account – Cost of Goods Sold.

ii) Name/Description – Sea Wind Carbon Sailboat, track quantity, initial quantity 12/31/18 – 3, inventory asset account – Inventory Asset, price - $1,200, cost - $620, income account – Sales, expense account – Cost of Goods Sold.

b. Service - Name/Description – Repairs, rate – $45, income account – Services.

c. Make changes to the following accounts via journal entry 1 as of 12/31/18 with an offset to Opening Balance Equity:

Account	Amount	Name
Accounts Receivable	925.00	Benson's RC (new customer)
Prepaid Expenses	2,400.00	
Accounts Payable	1,900.00	Kyosho (new vendor)

4 Close the Opening Balance Equity account to Retained Earnings via journal entry 2 as of 12/31/18.

5 Prepare and print a Trial Balance report as of 12/31/18, save it as a customized report named Trial Balance 12/31/18, and share it with all users. Your report should look like Figure 3.17.

Figure 3.17

Trial Balance (as of 12/31/18)

Case 2
TRIAL BALANCE
As of December 31, 2018

	DEBIT	CREDIT
Checking	5,000.00	
Accounts Receivable	925.00	
Inventory Asset	5,060.00	
Prepaid Expenses	2,400.00	
Machinery & Equipment:Depreciation		1,000.00
Machinery & Equipment:Original cost	10,000.00	
Accounts Payable		1,900.00
Notes Payable		12,000.00
Common Stock		100.00
Opening Balance Equity		0.00
Retained Earnings		8,385.00
TOTAL	$23,385.00	$23,385.00

6 If your trial balance is differ from what is in Figure 3.17, do the following:

a. Make sure all of your changes were dated 12/31/18.

b. Click on the debit or credit balance to view a transactions report for each account, and investigate why your answer is different.

c. Ask you instructor for assistance.

d. Be sure your company matches the above since, in the following chapter, you will be adding additional business events.

7   Export your Trial Balance report to Excel, and save it with the file name: Student Name (replace with your name) Ch 03 Case 02 Trial Balance.xlsx.

8   Prepare and print a Transaction Detail by Account report for all transactions between 1/1/2010 and 12/31/2020, save it as a customized report named Transaction Detail by Account, and share it with all users. If asked, indicate that your business is accrual based.

9   Use your Transaction Detail by Account report to locate any differences in your Trial Balance report created above.

   a.   Make sure all of your changes were dated 12/31/18.

   b.   Click on the line that does not match to view the transaction for that account, and investigate why your answer differs.

   c.   Ask you instructor for assistance.

   d.   Be sure your company matches the above since, in the following chapter, you will be adding additional business events.

10 Export your Transactions Detail by Account report to Excel and save it with the file name: Student Name (replace with your name) Ch 03 Case 02 Transaction Detail by Account.xlsx.

11 Sign out of your company.

Operating Activities: Sales and Cash Receipts

Student Learning Outcomes

Upon completion of this chapter, the student will be able to do the following:

- Create a new service, product, and customer
- Record a sales receipt
- Record an invoice for services rendered on account
- Record an invoice for products sold on account
- Record cash receipts (payments received on account)
- Deposit payments received on account
- Prepare a Transaction Detail by Account report

Overview

Intuit has provided a Sample Company online to provide new users a test drive of its QBO product. In this chapter, you will open this Sample Company and practice various features of QBO. You will be recording operating activities, such as adding new services, new products, new customers, new sales receipts, new invoices, and new cash receipts to the Sample Company file. Remember, if you stop in the middle of this work, none of your work will be saved. So, when you return, the same Sample Company, without your work, will appear. In the end of chapter, you will perform the same tasks completed on the Sample Company on your Student Company. That work of course will be saved.

Services, Products, and Customers

In this section, you will add new services, products, and customers. To add new services and products, you will access the Company section using the **Gear** icon. To add customers, you will use the Customers menu item in the Navigation Bar.

To add new services, products and customers to the Sample Company, do the following:

1   Open your Internet browser.

2   Type **https://qbo.intuit.com/redir/testdrive** into your browser's address text box and the press [**Enter**] to view the Sample Company Home page. The system may ask you to provide security information before proceeding.

If so, type the words provided into the text box and then click **Continue**. Your system date will differ from the date shown under the company name in the figure below. Transaction dates may also differ on your screen from in the figures shown throughout this text.

3   Click the **Gear** icon, and click **Products and Services** shown in Figure 4.1.

Figure 4.1

List of Products and Services

4   Click **New** in the upper right-hand corner of the **Products and Services** list.

5   Click **Select a Product Type** and then select **Service**.

6   Type **Rose Consulting** in the **Name** text box and the **Description on sales forms** text boxes.

7   Check the **Sales Information** check box, and type **45** in the **Price/Rate** text box as shown in Figure 4.2.

8   Scroll down the window and accept Services as the Income account and then check the **Is taxable** check box neither of which is shown in Figure 4.2.

Figure 4.2

Product or Service Information
(adding a new service)

Product or Service Information   ×

Service ⬍

*Name

Rose Consulting

SKU

☐ Is sub-product/service

Enter parent product/se ⬍

Upload

Sales Information

☑ I sell this product/service to my customers

Description on sales forms

Rose Consulting

Price/Rate

45

Income account

Purchasing Information

☐ I purchase this product/service from a vendor

Cancel   Save and Close ⬍

9 Click on the drop-down arrow to the right of the **Save and Close** button, and select **Save and New**.

GO BACK TO PRODUCT TYPE

10 Click **Select a Product Type** and then select ~~Item~~. *INVENTORY*

11 Type **Roses** in the **Name** text box and check the **Tract Quantity** check box.

NOT THERE

12 Type **0** in the **Initial Quantity On Hand** text box and type today's date in the **As Of Date** text box.

13 Select **Inventory Asset** as the Inventory Asset Account.

14 Type **Roses** in the **Sale Information** and in **Purchasing Information** text boxes.

15 Type **25** in the **Price/Rate** text box and **15** in the **Cost** text box.

16 Select **Sales of Product Income** from the Income Account drop-down list and **Cost of Goods Sold** from the Expense Account drop-down list.

ALREADY THERE

17 Check the **Is Taxable** check box. A partial view of the Product or Service Information window should look like Figure 4.3.

Figure 4.3

Product or Service Information (adding a new product)

18 Click on the drop-down arrow to the right of the **Save and New** button, and select **Save and Close**.

19 Scroll down the revised list of Products and Service to see the service and product you entered shown in Figure 4.4.

AT BOTTOM

Figure 4.4

Updated List of Products and Services (partial view)

20 Click the **Customers** menu in the Navigation Bar, and click the **New Customer** button.

21 Type **James** and in the **First name** text box and **Roxy** in the **Last name** text box.

22 Type **Roxy Corp.** in the **Company** and in the **Display name as** text boxes.

23 Select the **Address** tab, and type **101 Ocean View**, **La Jolla**, **CA**, **92130** in the appropriate text boxes.

24 Select the **Payment and billing** tab, and select **Net 30** from the Terms text box. A partial view of the **Customer Information** window is shown in Figure 4.5

Figure 4.5

Customer Information window (partial view)

Customer Information

Title	First name	Middle name	Last name	Suffix
	James		Roxy	

Company

Roxy Corp.

*Display name as

Roxy Corp.

Print on check as ☑ Use display name

Roxy Corp.

25 Click **Save**.

26 The Roxy Corp. customer window appears shown in Figure 4.6.

Figure 4.6

Roxy Corp. (customer window)

You have now added a new service, a new product, and a new customer. Next up, adding sales receipts to record cash sales and invoices to record credit sales.

Sales Receipts and Invoices

A business uses sales receipts to record sales transactions on a daily basis where payment is received at the same time as a product or service is delivered. Sales invoices are used to record sales transactions where customers are granted credit terms and given some time to pay after a product or service is delivered. In either case, sales are recorded when the product or services are rendered.

To add sales receipts and invoices to the Sample Company, do the following:

1 Continue from where you left off. If you closed the Sample Company, follow the steps to re-open it found at the beginning of this chapter.

2 Click the **Create** (+) icon, and select **Sales Receipt** shown in Figure 4.7.

Figure 4.7

Create window (adding a sales receipt)

3 Select **Bill's Windsurf Shop** from the Choose a customer drop-down list in the upper left-hand corner of the Sales Receipt window.

4 Your computer's system date has been entered as the Sales Receipt date.

5 Select **Check** from the drop-down list of Payment methods.

6 The check will be recorded in the Undeposited Funds account since deposits for this company are made every other day.

7 On line 1 of the sales receipt, select **Pump** from the drop-down list of Products/Services.

8 Type **2** in the QTY (Quantity) column.

9 On line 2 of the sales receipt, select **Rock Fountain** from the drop-down list of Products/Services.

10 Type **2** in the QTY (Quantity) column and then press [**Tab**]. The sales receipt should look like Figure 4.8.

Figure 4.8

Sales Receipt before Sales Tax (partial view)

11 Scroll down the sales receipt, and select **California** from the drop-down list in the **Select a sales tax rate** text box. The lower half of your sales receipt should look like Figure 4.9 with the $46.40 tax amount added.

Figure 4.9

Sales Receipt after Sales Tax (partial view)

12 Click **Save and Close**.

13 Click the **Customers** menu item from the Navigation Bar, and click **Bill's Windsurf Shop**. A listing of recent transactions affecting that customer are shown, including the recorded sales receipt shown in Figure 4.10.

Figure 4.10

Bill's Windsurf Shop (recent transactions)

14 Click the **Create (+)** icon, and select **Invoice** shown in Figure 4.11.

Figure 4.11

Create windows (adding an invoice)

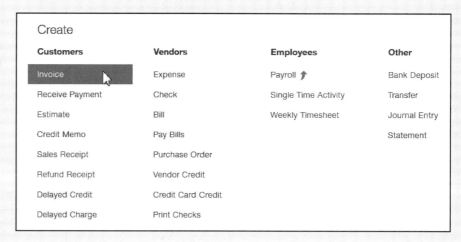

15   Select **Cool Cars** from the Choose a customer drop-down list in the upper left-hand corner of the Invoice window.

16   Your computer's system date has been entered as the Invoice date, and the default terms for this customer are in the appropriate text boxes.

17   On line 1 of the invoice, select **Trimming** from the drop-down list of Products/Services.

18   Type **5** in the Quantity (QTY) column.

19   On line 2 of the sales receipt, select **Pest Control** from the drop-down list of Products/Services.

20   Type **3** in the Quantity (QTY) column and then press [**Tab**]. The invoice should look like Figure 4.12.

Figure 4.12

Invoice (partial view)

21   Scroll down the invoice and select **California** from the drop-down list in the Select a sales tax rate text box. Even though a rate is selected, no sales tax is applied. Both services are not taxable, and thus, no sales tax is added.

22   Click **Save and Close**.

23   Click the **Customers** menu item from the Navigation Bar and then click **Cool Cars**. A listing of recent transactions affecting that customer are shown, including the recorded invoice shown in Figure 4.13.

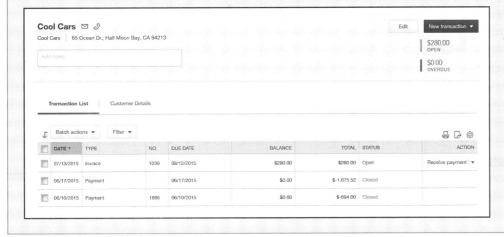

Figure 4.13

Cool Cars (recent transactions)

Cash Receipts

In QBO, the concept of cash receipts is referred to as receiving payments. Thus, to record the receipt of payment from a customer, you can use the Receive Payment item in the Create (+) icon to record the transaction, or you can use Receive Payment from the Action column in a customer's list of transactions. Once a payment is received, it must be deposited into your bank account. This is a separate but important process in QBO.

To record the receipt of a payment to the Sample Company from a customer, do the following:

1 Continue from where you left off. If you closed the Sample Company, follow the steps to re-open it found at the beginning of this chapter.

2 Click the **Create (+)** icon, and select **Receive Payment** shown in Figure 4.14.

Figure 4.14

Create window (recording the receipt of a customer payment)

3 Select **Jeff's Jalopies** from the Choose a customer drop-down list in the upper left-hand corner of the Receive Payment window.

4 Your computer's system date has been entered as the Payment date.

5 Select **Check** as the Payment method. The Undeposited Funds account will be used to record this check.

6 Place a check in the **Invoice # 1022** check box shown in Figure 4.15 (Do not click Save.)

Figure 4.15

Receive Payment window

CLEAR PAYMENT

7   Click **Cancel** so you can explore the other means of recording this transaction. Click **Yes** when asked if you want to leave without saving.

8   Click the **Customers** menu item from the Navigation Bar, and click **Jeff's Jalopies**. A listing of recent transactions affecting that customer are shown including invoice # 1022 shown in Figure 4.16.

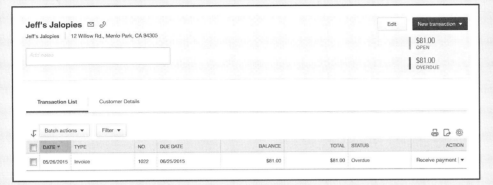

Figure 4.16

Jeff's Jalopies Recent Transactions

9   Click **Receive payment** in the Action column next to invoice # 1022.

10   The same Receive Payment window you saw before reappears. Thus, you have two ways of accessing and recording the receipt of payments from a customer. Enter the same information you did above as shown in Figure 4.15, and click **Save and Close**.

✓ ALREADY THERE

11   In the Jeff's Jalopies window, the transactions and payment are shown, and the balance is $0.00 shown in Figure 4.17.

Figure 4.17

Jeff's Jalopies window (recent transactions)

12   Click the **Create (+)** icon, and select **Bank Deposit** from the Other column shown in Figure 4.18.

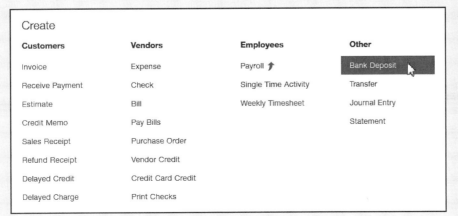

Figure 4.18

Create window (inputting a bank deposit)

13 Select the payment received from Freeman Sporting Goods from the list of existing payments shown in Figure 4.19.

Figure 4.19

Deposit window

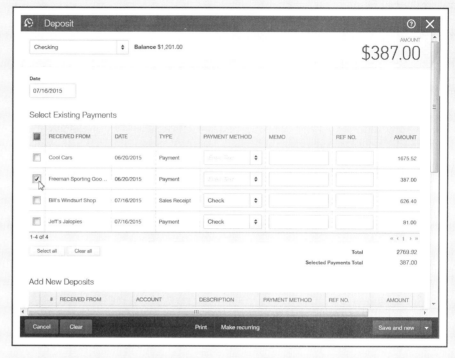

14 Click **Save and Close**.

Transaction Detail by Account

In the cases found at the end of each chapter, you will be asked to create a Trial Balance report as of a certain date. You will compare your Trial Balance report with one provided in the case to see if you have correctly recorded various business events. If your Trial Balance differs, you will need to fix your errors.

A usual explanation for an incorrect Trial Balance report is recording a transaction in an incorrect period, not recording it at all, or recording it incorrectly. To investigate, you will need to create a transaction detail by account report for a specific period. You can create such a report for all transactions to see if yours were recorded in the proper period and to see where you may have entered a wrong amount or account.

To create, print, and export a transaction detail by account report for all transactions, do the following:

1 Continue from your work above. (If you do not, none of your work in this chapter will be visible since it is not saved for the Sample Company.)

2 Click **Reports** from the Navigation bar.

3 Type **Transaction** in the Go to Report text box.

4   Select **Transaction Detail by Account**.

5   Select **All Dates** from the Transaction Date drop-down text box.

6   Click **Run Report**. The top of the report is shown in Figure 4.20.

[handwritten: GET RID OF DROP-DOWN BOX]

Craig's Design and Landscaping Services
TRANSACTION DETAIL BY ACCOUNT
All Dates

DATE	TRANSACTION TYPE	NUM	NAME	MEMO/DESCRIPTION	SPLIT	AMOUNT	BALANCE
Checking							
02/04/2015	Deposit			Opening Balance	Opening Balance Equity	5,000.00	5,000.00
03/18/2015	Bill Payment (Check)	10	Robertson & Associates		Accounts Payable (A/P)	-300.00	4,700.00
03/26/2015	Payment	1053	Bill's Windsurf Shop		Accounts Receivable (A/R)	175.00	4,875.00
04/09/2015	Expense	12	Robertson & Associates		Legal & Professional Fees:Accounting	-250.00	4,625.00
05/01/2015	Check	4	Chin's Gas and Oil		Automobile:Fuel	-54.55	4,570.45
05/07/2015	Sales Tax Payment			Q1 Payment	-Split-	-38.50	4,531.95
05/07/2015	Sales Tax Payment			Q1 Payment	-Split-	-38.40	4,493.55
05/10/2015	Expense	9	Tania's Nursery		Job Expenses:Job Materials:Plants and Soil	-89.09	4,404.46
05/10/2015	Check	12	Books by Bessie		Legal & Professional Fees:Bookkeeper	-55.00	4,349.46
05/16/2015	Check	5	Chin's Gas and Oil		Automobile:Fuel	-62.01	4,287.45

Figure 4.20

Transaction Detail by Account report (top section)

7   Scroll down the report until you locate the deposit you recorded from Freeman Sporting Goods shown in Figure 4.21.

[handwritten: PAYMENT 12/17 5664]

			masonry				
06/19/2015	Bill Payment (Check)	6	PG&E		Accounts Payable (A/P)	-114.09	1,560.10
06/20/2015	Deposit				-Split-	868.15	2,428.25
06/20/2015	Expense	76	Pam Seitz		Legal & Professional Fees	-75.00	2,353.25
06/20/2015	Check	75	Hicks Hardware		-Split-	-228.75	2,124.50
06/23/2015	Cash Expense		Tania's Nursery		Job Expenses:Job Materials:Plants and Soil	-23.50	2,101.00
07/04/2015	Credit Card Credit				Mastercard	-900.00	1,201.00
07/16/2015	Deposit			Freeman Sporting Goods:0969 Ocean View Road	Undeposited Funds	387.00	1,588.00
Total for Checking							$1,588.00

Figure 4.21

Transaction Detail by Account report (partial view)

8   Click on ~~Deposit~~ for Freeman Sporting Goods to view the deposit recorded. *[handwritten: PAYMENT]*

9   Close this window, scroll down the report, and investigate other transactions.

10   Scroll back to the top of this report, and click **Save Customization**. *[handwritten: GREEN BOX AT RIGHT]*

11   Place a check in the **Share this report with all company users** check box, and click ~~OK.~~ *[handwritten: SAVE]*   *[handwritten: SHARE WITH ALL]*

12   Click the **Print** button to set this report up for printing; however, do not print this report since it is too long and unnecessary. Click **Cancel**. *[handwritten: SEND TO INSTRUCTOR]*

13   Click the **Gear** icon, and click **Sign Out**.

This report can help identifying and correcting errors.

End Note

You have now added a customer, product, and service. You have recorded a sales receipt, invoice, payment received from a customer, and deposit to a bank account. These are operating activities. Additional operating activities related to purchases and cash payments follow in the next chapter.

Chapter 4 Questions

1 What steps need to be followed to add a new product or service?

2 What steps need to be followed to record a new sales receipt?

3 What steps need to be followed to record a new invoice?

4 What steps need to be followed to record a new payment from a customer?

5 What steps need to be followed to record a new deposit to the bank?

6 What are the differences between adding a new product and adding a new service?

7 What is the difference between a sales receipt and a sales invoice?

Chapter 4 Matching

a. Invoice   _____ A service in the Sample Company

b. Sales receipt   _____ Providing the bank a payment from a customer

c. Product   _____ Used when recording a sale on account

d. Service   _____ Used to access invoices, sales receipts, or bank deposits

e. Create (+) icon   _____ A customer in the Sample Company

f. Payment from a customer   _____ Quantities of this are not tracked

g. Deposit   _____ Used when cash is collected at the time of a sale

h. Pest control   _____ Cash receipts received from a sale

i. Roses   _____ Quantities of this are tracked

j. Cool Cars   _____ A product in the Sample Company

Chapter 4 Cases

The following cases require you to open the company you updated in Chapter 3. Each case below continues throughout the text in a sequential manner. For example, if you are assigned Case 1, you will use the file you modified in this chapter in all following chapters. Each case below is similar in concepts assessed but differs in amounts and transactions.

To reopen your company, do the following:

1 Open your Internet browser.

2 Type **https://qbo.intuit.com/qbo28/login?webredir** into your browser's address text box.

3 Type your User ID and Password into the text boxes as you have done before.

Case 1

Add some operating activities (sales and cash receipts) to your company.

Based on what you learned in the text and using the Sample Company, you are to add the following transactions to your company:

1   Add a new customer – Name: Sarah Hay, Company: Hey Hays Surf, Display name as: Sarah Hay, Address: 230 Beach Way, La Jolla, CA, 92039

2   Add a new service – Tune-Up, Rate: $85.00, income account: Services.

3   Add a new product with quantity tracked – Fred Rubble, initial quantity on hand: 0, as of date 1/1/2018, price: $950.00, cost: $600.00, income account: Sales, expense account: Cost of Goods Sold.

4   Record a new sales receipt on 1/3/18 – Customer: Blondie's Boards, payment method: Check, reference no.: 893, deposit to: Undeposited Funds, product: Rook 15, quantity: 2

5   Record a new invoice on 1/4/18 – Customer: Hey Hays Surf, terms: Net 30, service: Tune-Up, quantity: 2, product: The Water Hog, quantity: 1

6   Record a new cash payment received on 1/5/18 – Customer: Blondie's Boards, payment method: Check, reference no.: 984, deposit to: Undeposited Funds, amount received: $5,000.00

7   Record a deposit made on 1/8/18 to the checking account – Received from: Blondie's Boards, amount received: $1,300.00, related to: Sales Receipt.

8   Prepare a Trial Balance report with a From date of 1/1/18 and a To date of 1/31/18, save it as a customized report named Trial Balance 1/31/18, and share it with all users. Your report should look like Figure 4.22. If asked, indicate that your business is accrual based.

Figure 4.22

Trial Balance (as of 1/31/18)

Case 1
TRIAL BALANCE
As of January 31, 2018

	DEBIT	CREDIT
Checking	26,300.00	
Accounts Receivable	1,030.00	
Inventory Asset	6,700.00	
Prepaid Expenses	3,000.00	
Undeposited Funds	5,000.00	
Furniture & Fixtures:Depreciation		10,000.00
Furniture & Fixtures:Original cost	40,000.00	
Accounts Payable		4,500.00
Notes Payable		60,000.00
Common Stock		1,000.00
Opening Balance Equity		0.00
Retained Earnings		5,500.00
Sales		2,160.00
Services		170.00
Cost of Goods Sold	1,300.00	
TOTAL	**$83,330.00**	**$83,330.00**

9 If your trial balance differs from what is in Figure 4.22, do the following:

   a. Make sure that all of your changes were dated in January 2018.

   b. Click on the debit or credit balance to view a transactions report for each account, and investigate why your answer differs.

   c. Ask you instructor for assistance.

   d. Be sure your company matches the above since, in the following chapter, you will add additional business events.

10 Export your Trial Balance report to Excel, and save it with the file name: Student Name (replace with your name) Ch 04 Case 01 Trial Balance.xlsx.

11 Open and print the custom report you created in the last chapter called Transaction Detail by Account.

12 Use your Transaction Detail by Account report to locate any differences in your Trial Balance report created above.

   a. Make sure all of your changes were dated in January 2018.

   b. Click on the line that does not match to view the transaction for that account, and investigate why your answer differs.

   c. Ask you instructor for assistance.

   d. Be sure your company matches the above since, in the following chapter, you will add additional business events.

13 Export your Transactions Detail by Account report to Excel and save it with the file name: Student Name (replace with your name) Ch 04 Case 01 Transaction Detail by Account.xlsx.

14 Sign out of your company.

Case 2

Add some operating activities (sales and cash receipts) to your company. Based on what you learned in the text and using the Sample Company, you are to add the following transactions:

1 Add a new customer – Hagen's Toys, 3983 Torrey Pines, La Jolla, CA, 92039

2 Add a new service – Custom Painting, Rate: $45.00, income account: Services.

3 Add 2 new products with quantity tracked – GO Aircraft Radio, initial quantity on hand: 0, as of date 1/1/2019, price: $4,999.00, cost: $2,500.00, income account: Sales, expense account: Cost of Goods Sold and Taylor 22cc, initial quantity on hand: 0, as of date 1/1/2019, price: $2,999.00, cost: $1,500.00, income account: Sales, expense account: Cost of Goods Sold.

4 Record a new sales receipt on 1/3/19 – Customer: Benson's RC, payment method: Credit Card, reference no.: 16756, deposit to: Undeposited Funds, product: Broon F830 Ride, quantity: 3

5 Record a new invoice on 1/4/19 – Customer: Hagen's Toys, terms: Net 30, service: Custom Painting, quantity: 5, product: Seawind Carbon Sailboat, quantity: 1

6 Record a new cash payment received on 1/7/19 – Customer: Benson's RC, payment method: Check, reference no.: 9847, deposit to: Undeposited Funds, amount received: $925.00

7 Record a deposit made on 1/7/19 to the checking account – Received from: Benson's RC, amount received: $4,500.00, related to: Sales Receipt.

8 Prepare a Trial Balance report with a From date of 1/1/19 and a To date of 1/31/19, save it as a customized report named Trial Balance 1/31/19, and share it with all users. Your report should look like Figure 4.23. If asked, indicate that your business is accrual based.

Figure 4.23

Trial Balance (as of 1/31/19)

Case 2
TRIAL BALANCE
As of January 31, 2019

	DEBIT	CREDIT
Checking	9,500.00	
Accounts Receivable	1,425.00	
Inventory Asset	2,040.00	
Prepaid Expenses	2,400.00	
Undeposited Funds	925.00	
Machinery & Equipment:Depreciation		1,000.00
Machinery & Equipment:Original cost	10,000.00	
Accounts Payable		1,900.00
Notes Payable		12,000.00
Common Stock		100.00
Opening Balance Equity		0.00
Retained Earnings		8,385.00
Sales		5,700.00
Services		225.00
Cost of Goods Sold	3,020.00	
TOTAL	$29,310.00	$29,310.00

9 If your trial balance differs from what is in Figure 4.23, do the following:

a. Make sure that all of your changes were dated in January 2019.

b. Click on the debit or credit balance to view a transactions report for each account, and investigate why your answer differs.

c. Ask you instructor for assistance.

d. Be sure your company matches the above since, in the following chapter, you will add additional business events.

10 Export your Trial Balance report to Excel and save it with the file name: Student Name (replace with your name) Ch 04 Case 02 Trial Balance.xlsx.

11 Open and print the custom report you created in the last chapter called Transaction Detail by Account.

12 Use your Transaction Detail by Account report to locate any differences in your Trial Balance report created above.

    a. Make sure that all of your changes were dated in January 2019.

    b. Click on the line that does not match to view the transaction for that account, and investigate why your answer differs.

    c. Ask you instructor for assistance.

    d. Be sure your company matches the above since, in the following chapter, you will add additional business events.

13 Export your Transactions Detail by Account report to Excel and save it with the file name: Student Name (replace with your name) Ch 04 Case 02 Transaction Detail by Account.xlsx.

14 Sign out of your company.

Operating Activities: Purchases and Cash Payments

Student Learning Outcomes

Upon completion of this chapter, the student will be able to do the following:

- Create a vendor
- Record a purchase order
- Record a bill for the receipt of products/services on account
- Record the payment of bills
- Record credit card charges
- Record checks
- Prepare a Trial Balance and drill-down to a transaction report for an account

Overview

Intuit has provided a sample company online to provide new users a test drive of its QBO product. In this chapter, you will open this sample company and practice various features of QBO. You will be recording operating activities, such as adding vendors, purchase orders, bills, bill payments, credit card charges, and checks to the Sample Company file. Remember, if you stop in the middle of this work, none of your work will be saved. So, when you return, the same Sample Company, without your work, will appear. In the end of chapter work, you will be asked to perform the same tasks completed on the Sample Company on your Student Company. That work, of course, will be saved.

Vendors

In this section you will be adding new vendors. Recall that vendors are your company's suppliers of products and services. To add vendors you will use the Vendors menu item in the Navigation Bar.

To add new vendors to the Sample Company, do the following:

1 Open your Internet browser.

2 Type **https://qbo.intuit.com/redir/testdrive** into your browser's address text box, and then press [**Enter**] to view the Sample Company Home page.

3 Click the **Vendor** menu in the Navigation Bar, and click the **New Vendor** button.

4 Type **Valley Rock** in the **Company** and the **Display name as** text boxes.

5 Type the address **290 Central Ave.**, **Middletown**, **CA**, **94482** in the appropriate text boxes.

6 Select **Net 30** from the Terms text box. A Vendor Information window is shown in Figure 5.1

Figure 5.1

Vendor Information window

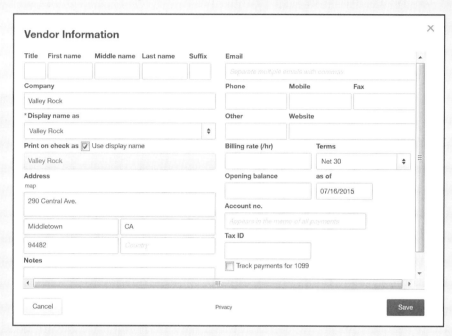

7 Click **Save**.

You have added a new vendor. Next up, adding purchase orders.

Purchase Orders

A business uses purchase orders to formally order products or services from its vendors. Purchase orders are also used as a reference and control for products received. During the creation of a purchase order, you can create a new product. Purchase orders can be for inventory or for products ordered for a specific customer.

To add two purchase orders and new product to the Sample Company, do the following:

1 Continue from where you left off above.

2 Click the **Create** (+) icon, and select **Purchase Order** as shown in Figure 5.2.

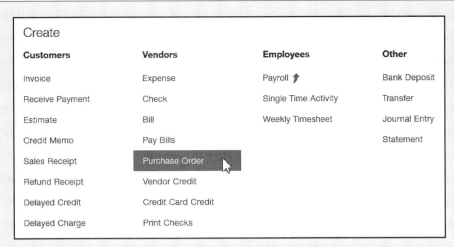

Figure 5.2

Create windows (adding a purchase order)

3 Select **Valley Rock** from the Choose a vendor drop-down list in the upper left-hand corner of the Purchase Order window.

4 Your computer's system date has been entered as the purchase order date.

5 Click in the **Product/Service** column on line 1 of the purchase order's Item details section, and select **Add New** shown in Figure 5.3.

Figure 5.3

Purchase Order (adding a new product)

6 Create a new product, as you've done before – product type: ~~Item,~~ *INVENTORY* name and description: **Landscape Rock**, tracking quantity on hand, initial quantity on hand: **0**, inventory asset account: **Inventory Asset**, price: **75**, cost: **50**, income account: **Sales of Product Income**, expense account: **Cost of Goods Sold**, is taxable: **yes**. Click **Save and Close**.

7 Type **100** in the Quantity (QTY) column. Leave the Customer field blank as this order is for inventory. Your completed purchase order should look like Figure 5.4.

Figure 5.4

Purchase Order (for Valley Rock)

8 Click ~~**Save and New.**~~ *SAVE AND SEND*
SEND AND CLOSE

9 Select **Hicks Hardware** from the Choose a vendor drop-down list in the upper left-hand corner of the Purchase Order window.

10 The Item details section of the purchase order is filled out with information from the last purchase order completed for this vendor. Leave all lines of the Product/Service column as is.

11 Change the amounts in the Quantity (QTY) column as follows: Rock Fountain **3**, Sprinkler Heads **20**, Sprinkler Pipes **30**, and Pump **4**.

12 Select **Kookies by Kathy** in the Customer column for all four items so your purchase order looks like Figure 5.5.

Figure 5.5

Purchase Order
(to Hicks Hardware)

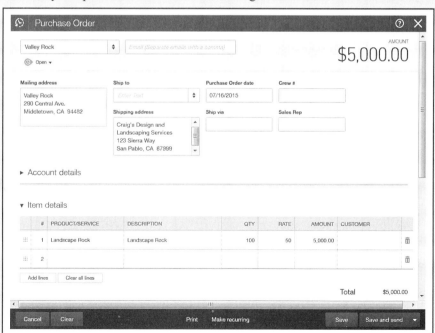

13 Click **Save and Close**.

Bills

In the previous chapter, you created invoices to customers for products or services rendered. That invoice served as a bill to that customer signifying a sales transaction for you and a bill to them. Likewise, when you enter into a business transaction, such as purchasing a product or service from a vendor, you expect them to send you an invoice. In QBO, the invoice you receive from a vendor is called a bill. Bills are recorded in QBO to signify the receipt of a product or service and a related liability, usually accounts payable. The inventory account is affected when the bill represents a product being delivered.

In QBO, the terms of those bills could be one of the following: due on receipt, net 10, net 15, net 30, or net 60. The net reference means the bill is due to be paid within a specified number of days, for example, 10, 15, 30, or 60 days. Other terms, for example, 2/10 net 30, provide for a 2% discount on the invoice if paid within 10 days; otherwise, a payment is required within 30 days. Even though you can set up such terms to appear on invoices to customers and bills from vendors, QBO does not calculate them automatically. To simplify your learning of QBO, discounts have not been implemented in this text.

In this section, you will focus on recording a bill for the receipt of services and products on account, meaning you will have been given terms (usually net 30), so you will not have to pay the bill for 30 days after the bill date. The first product purchased had been previously ordered using a purchase order. The second product ordered is a new product, which had not been previously ordered using a purchase order. Both of these purchases will affect inventory and are, thus, recorded in the Items detail section of a bill. The third transaction is a service that was rendered and does not affect inventory and is, therefore, recorded in the Accounts detail section of a bill.

To record a bill from a vendor for the receipt of products/services on account, do the following:

1 Continue from where you left off.

2 Click the **Create** (+) icon, and click **Bill** in the Vendor column shown in Figure 5.6.

Figure 5.6

Create window (entering bills)

Create			
Customers	**Vendors**	**Employees**	**Other**
Invoice	Expense	Payroll ⭧	Bank Deposit
Receive Payment	Check	Single Time Activity	Transfer
Estimate	Bill	Weekly Timesheet	Journal Entry
Credit Memo	Pay Bills		Statement
Sales Receipt	Purchase Order		
Refund Receipt	Vendor Credit		
Delayed Credit	Credit Card Credit		
Delayed Charge	Print Checks		

3 Select **Tim Phillip Masonry** from the Choose a vendor drop-down list.

4 Select **Net 30** from the drop-down list of terms.

5 Collapse the Account details section of the bill by clicking on the arrow next to **Account details**.

6 Expand the Item details section of the bill by clicking on the arrow next to **Item details**.

7 Click **Add** in the Add to Bill section, which identifies an open purchase order #1002 from this vendor located on the right of the bill shown in Figure 5.7.

Figure 5.7

Bill (adding purchase order information)

8 Collapse the Account details section of the bill by clicking on the arrow next to **Account details**.

9 The purchase order contains information from purchase order #1002 shown in Figure 5.8.

Figure 5.8

Bill (after purchase order information is added)

10 Click **Save and New**.

11   Select **Tania's Nursery** from the Choose a vendor drop-down list.

12   Select **Net 30** from the drop-down list of terms.

13   Select **Add new** on line 1 of the bill in the Product/Service column.

14   Add a new product (which you will track quantities) as you have done before – product type: **Item**, name and description: **Lavender**, initial quantity on hand: **0**, inventory asset account: **Inventory Asset**, price: **15**, cost: **10**, income account: **Sales of Product Income,** expense account: **Cost of Goods Sold,** is taxable: **yes**.

15   Type **100** on line 1 of the bill in the Quantity (QTY) column

16   Click **Save and New**.

17   Select **Computers by Jenni** from the Choose a vendor drop-down list.

18   Select **Net 30** from the drop-down list of terms.

19   Expand the Account details section of the bill by clicking on the **arrow next to Account details**.

20   Collapse the Item details section of the bill by clicking on the **arrow next to Item details**.

21   Select **Equipment Rental** on line 1 of the bill in the Account column.

22   Type **1200** on line 1 of the bill in the Amount column shown in Figure 5.9.

Figure 5.9

Bill (for services)

23   Click **Save and New**.

24   Select **Brosnahan Insurance Agency** from the Choose a vendor drop-down list.

25   Accept **Net 10** from the drop-down list of terms.

26   The bill information is filled in automatically based on the last bill entered for this vendor.

27   Select **Prepaid Expenses** on line 1 of the bill in the Account column replacing Insurance

28   Type **1800** on line 1 of the bill in the Amount column replacing the existing amount shown in Figure 5.10.

Figure 5.10

Bill for Prepaid Expenses (recording)

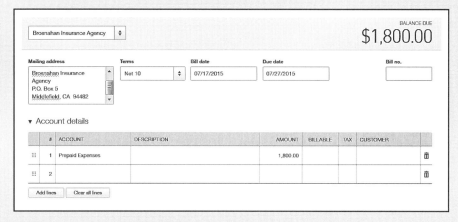

29   Click **Save and Close**.

All bills entered increased an asset or an expense account. Inventory purchases were all recorded in the Item details section and increased the quantity of those products (as long as they were originally set up as "tracked" products). Equipment rental was recorded as an expense and the prepaid insurance was recorded as an asset (Prepaid Expenses). All bills increased the accounts payable liability account.

Payment of Bills, Use of a Credit Card, Payments for Items Other than Bills

In this section, you will focus on recording the payment of a bill for the receipt of services and/or products on account, recording credit card charges, or recording the payment by check for other items.

To pay bills, do the following:

1   Continue from where you left off.

2   Click the **Create** (+) icon, and click **Pay Bills** in the Vendor column shown in Figure 5.11.

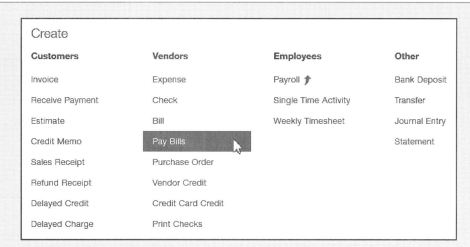

Figure 5.11

Create window (paying bills)

3   A listing of possible bills that can be paid appears. In the Pay Bills window, select **Checking** from the drop-down list in the Payment Account box shown in Figure 5.12.

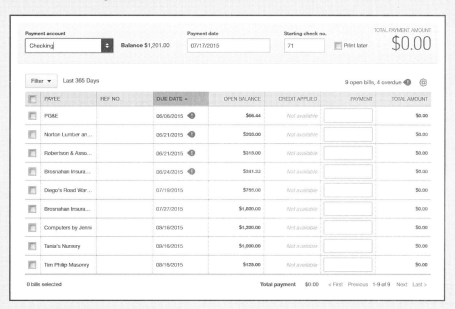

Figure 5.12

Bills to Pay

4   Click and hold your mouse between the PAYEE and REF NO. columns and drag to the right to increase the width of the PAYEE column.

5   Click and hold your mouse between the REF NO. and DUE DATE columns and drag to the left to decrease the width of the REF NO. column.

6   Click in the check box of payees PG&E, Norton Lumber and Building Materials, Robertson & Associates, and Brosnahan Insurance Agency shown in Figure 5.13.

Figure 5.13

Bills to Pay (selecting)

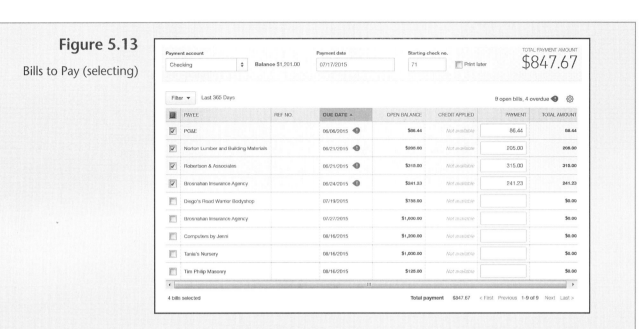

7   Click **Save and Close**.

You have now paid bills for products/services received for which you received a bill. However, often you will pay for a product/service or another expense for which you have not received a bill. Often, these are vendors, who give you no terms, and require you pay immediately. These terms are called due on receipt. For example, a credit card charge for fuel or a check for supplies. To record these transactions, you will use either the Expense task or the Check task after clicking the Create (+) icon. For ease of use, you will be directed to use the Expense task for all credit card transactions and the Check task for all checking account payments even though the Expense task can be used for either credit card charges or check payments.

To record a credit card or check payment, do the following:

1   Click the **Create (+)** icon.

2   Click **Expense** under the Vendor column.

3   Select **Chin's Gas and Oil** from the drop-down list in the **Choose a payee** text box.

4   Select **Mastercard** from the drop-down list in the **Choose an account** text box.

5   Accept **Automobile:Fuel** in the row 1 Account column and then type **85.00** as the amount replacing the existing 52.56 shown in Figure 5.14.

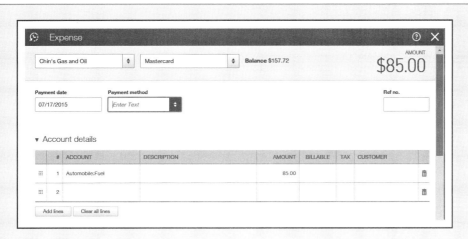

Figure 5.14

Credit Card Charge

6 Click **Save and Close**.

7 Click the **Create (+)** icon.

8 Click **Check** under the Vendor column.

9 Select **Cal Telephone** from the drop-down list in the **Choose a payee** text box.

10 Select **Checking** from the drop-down list in the **Choose an account** text box (it should be selected)

11 Type **77** in the **Check no.** text box.

12 Type **Utilities:Telephone** in the row 1 Account column, and type **325.00** as the amount shown in Figure 5.15.

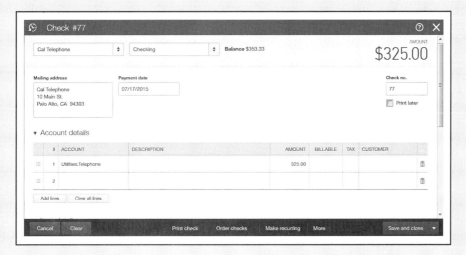

Figure 5.15

Check #77 (payment)

13 Click **Save and Close**.

Trial Balance

The work you completed in this chapter had an effect on the company's trial balance. You decided to create a Trial Balance report and investigate the checking, inventory asset, and accounts payable accounts. In the process, you realized that purchase orders do not affect a company's accounts until products are received or services are rendered.

Trouble? Recall the previous discussion of dates and amounts when using the Sample company. Dates in the text figures will be different than what you see in QBO when using the Sample company. Ending balances may also be different as they will all depend on what actual date you are entering transactions. Focus on the process rather than the resulting report dates or balances. This will not be the situation when you work on the end-of-chapter cases as those dates have been specifically identified.

To create a trial balance and investigate some account activity, do the following:

1   Click **Reports,** type **Trial Balance** into the Go to report text box, and press [**Enter**]. The upper portion of that report is shown in Figure 5.16.

Figure 5.16

Trial Balance (upper portion)

	DEBIT	CREDIT
Checking	28.33	
Savings	800.00	
Accounts Receivable (A/R)	5,281.52	
Inventory Asset	1,721.25	
Prepaid Expenses	1,800.00	
Undeposited Funds	2,062.52	
Truck:Original Cost	13,495.00	
Accounts Payable (A/P)		4,880.00
Mastercard		242.72
Arizona Dept. of Revenue Payable		0.00
Board of Equalization Payable		370.94
Loan Payable		4,000.00
Notes Payable		25,000.00

2   Click the Checking account balance of **28.33** to produce a Transaction Report for the Checking Account. The four bill payment checks you recorded earlier in this chapter and the check payment to Cal Telephone are shown in Figure 5.17.

Figure 5.17

Transaction Report (for the checking account)

Craig's Design and Landscaping Services
TRANSACTION REPORT
July 1-17, 2015

DATE	TRANSACTION TYPE	NUM	NAME	MEMO/DESCRIPTION	ACCOUNT	SPLIT	AMOUNT	BALANCE
Checking								
Beginning Balance								2,101.00
07/07/2015	Credit Card Credit				Checking	Mastercard	-900.00	1,201.00
07/17/2015	Bill Payment (Check)	72	Norton Lumber and Building Materials	32980256	Checking	Accounts Payable (A/P)	-205.00	996.00
07/17/2015	Bill Payment (Check)	74	Brosnahan Insurance Agency	7653412	Checking	Accounts Payable (A/P)	-241.23	754.77
07/17/2015	Check	77	Cal Telephone		Checking	Utilities:Telephone	-325.00	429.77
07/17/2015	Bill Payment (Check)	71	PG&E	00649587213	Checking	Accounts Payable (A/P)	-86.44	343.33
07/17/2015	Bill Payment (Check)	73	Robertson & Associates	000005641	Checking	Accounts Payable (A/P)	-315.00	28.33

3 Click **Print** to print this report.

4 Click **Back to Summary Report**.

5 Click the Inventory Asset account balance of **1,721.25** to produce a Transaction Report for the Inventory Asset account. The two bills for product purchases you recorded earlier in this chapter are shown in Figure 5.18.

Figure 5.18

Transaction Report (for the Inventory Asset Account)

Craig's Design and Landscaping Services
TRANSACTION REPORT
July 1-17, 2015

DATE	TRANSACTION TYPE	NUM	NAME	MEMO/DESCRIPTION	ACCOUNT	SPLIT	AMOUNT	BALANCE
Inventory Asset								
Beginning Balance								596.25
07/17/2015	Bill		Tim Philip Masonry	Rock Fountain	Inventory Asset	Accounts Payable (A/P)	125.00	721.25
07/17/2015	Bill		Tania's Nursery	Lavender	Inventory Asset	Accounts Payable (A/P)	1,000.00	1,721.25
Total for Inventory Asset							$1,125.00	
TOTAL							$1,125.00	

6 Click **Print** to print this report.

7 Click **Back to Summary Report**.

8 Click the Accounts Payable (A/P) account balance of **4,880.00** to produce a Transaction Report for the Accounts Payable (A/P) account. The bills for product and service purchases and the bill payments you recorded earlier in this chapter are shown in Figure 5.19.

Figure 5.19

Transaction Report (for the Accounts Payable account)

Craig's Design and Landscaping Services
TRANSACTION REPORT
July 1-17, 2015

DATE	TRANSACTION TYPE	NUM	NAME	MEMO/DESCRIPTION	ACCOUNT	SPLIT	AMOUNT	BALANCE
Accounts Payable (A/P)								
Beginning Balance								1,602.67
07/17/2015	Bill Payment (Check)	74	Brosnahan Insurance Agency		Accounts Payable (A/P)	Checking	-241.23	1,361.44
07/17/2015	Bill Payment (Check)	73	Robertson & Associates		Accounts Payable (A/P)	Checking	-315.00	1,046.44
07/17/2015	Bill Payment (Check)	72	Norton Lumber and Building Materials		Accounts Payable (A/P)	Checking	-205.00	841.44
07/17/2015	Bill		Tim Philip Masonry		Accounts Payable (A/P)	Inventory Asset	125.00	966.44
07/17/2015	Bill		Brosnahan Insurance Agency		Accounts Payable (A/P)	Prepaid Expenses	1,800.00	2,766.44
07/17/2015	Bill		Computers by Jenni		Accounts Payable (A/P)	Equipment Rental	1,200.00	3,966.44
07/17/2015	Bill		Tania's Nursery		Accounts Payable (A/P)	Inventory Asset	1,000.00	4,966.44
07/17/2015	Bill Payment (Check)	71	PG&E		Accounts Payable (A/P)	Checking	-86.44	4,880.00
Total for Accounts Payable (A/P)							$3,277.33	
TOTAL							$3,277.33	

9 Click **Print** to print this report.

10 Click **Back to Summary Report**.

11 Click the **Gear** icon, and click **Sign Out**.

End Note

In this chapter, you added a vendor, a product, purchase orders, bills, payment of bills, a credit card purchase, and a check payment. You also produced a trial balance and drilled down through that trial balance to see the effect the bills and payment of bills affected accounts. In the next chapter, you will work with investing and financing activities.

Chapter 5 Questions

1 Why does a business use purchase orders?

2 Describe the steps to create a new product from within a purchase order.

3 What happens when you create a new purchase order to a vendor from whom you recently placed a different purchase order?

4 What accounts are affected when a bill from a vendor supplying you products is recorded?

5 What appears when you click Pay Bills after clicking the Create (+) icon?

6 Describe the process for increasing or decreasing the width of a column in the listing of bills to pay.

7 What are the steps to record a credit card charge?

8 What are the steps to record a check written to pay something other than bills?

9 What are the steps to view a transaction report for the checking account from a trial balance?

10 What are the steps to view a transaction report for the inventory account from a trial balance?

Chapter 5 Matching

a. Purchase order

b. Due on receipt

c. Bill

d. Net 30

e. Item detail section

f. Account detail section

g. Pay Bills

h. Check

i. Expense

j. Vendor

_____ Purchases that affect inventory are recorded here

_____ An invoice sent by a vendor to a customer

_____ Purchases that don't affect inventory are recorded here

_____ Task used to record checks in the checking account

_____ Suppliers of products and services

_____ A formal means to order products from vendors

_____ Pay a bill within 30 days after the bill date

_____ Task used to record credit card charges

_____ Terms that provide no credit

_____ Paying vendors who have billed you

Chapter 5 Cases

The following cases require you to open the company you updated in Chapter 4. Each case below continues throughout the text in a sequential manner. For example, if you are assigned Case 1, you will use the file you modified in this chapter in all following chapters. Each case below is similar in concepts assessed but differs in amounts and transactions.

To reopen your company, do the following:

1   Open your Internet browser.

2   Type **https://qbo.intuit.com/qbo28/login?webredir** into your browser's address text box.

3   Type your User ID and Password into the text boxes as you have done before.

Case 1

Add some operating activities (purchases, credit card charges, and cash payments) to your company.

Based on what you learned in the text and using the Sample Company, you will add the following transactions to your company:

1   Add a new vendor – **Stewart Surfboards**, 2102 S El Camino Real, San Clemente, CA 92672 terms: net 30.

2   Add a new vendor – **Village Travel**, 100 S El Camino Real, San Clemente, CA 92672 terms: due on receipt.

3   Add a new vendor – **Office Depot**, 101 Main St., San Diego, CA 92600 terms: due on receipt.

4   Add a new account – Category type: **Credit Card,** detail type: **Credit Card**, name: **VISA**

5   Add a new account – Category type: **Other Current Assets**, detail type: **Other Current Assets**, name: **Supplies Asset**.

6   Add a new tracked product – Name/description: **California Nose Rider**, initial quantity on hand: **0**, inventory asset account: **Inventory Asset**, price: **3,200.00**, cost: **1,700.00**, income account: **Sales**, expense account: **Cost of Goods Sold**

7   Add a new tracked product – Name/description: **808**, initial quantity on hand: **0**, inventory asset account: **Inventory Asset,** price: **2,700.00**, cost: **1,500.00**, income account: **Sales**, expense account: **Cost of Goods Sold**

8   Record a new purchase order for products on **1/2/18** – Vendor: **Channel Islands**, product 1: **Fred Rubble**, QTY: **5**, product 2: **Rook 15**, QTY: **4**, product 3**: The Water Hog**, QTY: **1**

9   Record a new purchase order for products on **1/3/18** – Vendor: **Stewart Surfboards**, product 1: **808**, QTY: **2**, product 2: **California Nose Rider**, QTY: **1**

10   Record a new bill based on a purchase order #1001 on **1/5/18** – Vendor: **Channel Islands**, terms: **Net 15**. All items ordered were received.

11   Record a new bill without a purchase order on **1/8/18** – New vendor: **San Diego Gas & Electric**, terms: **Net 15**, account: **Utilities**, amount: **145.00**.

12   Record a new bill without a purchase order on **1/9/18** – New vendor: **Prime Properties**, terms: **Net 15**, account 1: **Rent or Lease**, amount: **2,500.00**, account 2: **Prepaid Expenses**, amount: **5,000.00**

13   Pay all bills due to **Channel Islands** on **1/19/18** using the checking account and starting with check no. 1001.

14   Record a credit card charge on **1/10/18,** vendor**: Village Travel**, using credit card: **VISA**, account: **Travel**, amount: **1,800.00**.

15   Record check on **1/11/18**, no.: **1002**, vendor: **Office Depot**, amount: **375.00**, account: **Supplies Asset**.

16   Open your previously customized report named Trial Balance 1/31/18. If a cash or accrual message appears just close the message. Your report should look like Figure 5.20.

Case 1

TRIAL BALANCE

As of January 31, 2018

	DEBIT	CREDIT
Checking	16,325.00	
Accounts Receivable	1,030.00	
Inventory Asset	11,800.00	
Prepaid Expenses	8,000.00	
Supplies Asset	375.00	
Undeposited Funds	5,000.00	
Furniture & Fixtures:Depreciation		10,000.00
Furniture & Fixtures:Original cost	40,000.00	
Accounts Payable		7,645.00
VISA		1,800.00
Notes Payable		60,000.00
Common Stock		1,000.00
Opening Balance Equity		0.00
Retained Earnings		5,500.00
Sales		2,160.00
Services		170.00
Cost of Goods Sold	1,300.00	
Rent or Lease	2,500.00	
Travel	1,800.00	
Utilities	145.00	
TOTAL	$88,275.00	$88,275.00

Figure 5.20

Trial Balance (as of 1/31/18)

17   Create and print a Transaction Report for the Checking account as you did earlier in the chapter.

18   Create and print a Transaction Report for the Inventory Asset account as you did earlier in the chapter.

19   Create and print a Transaction Report for the Accounts Payable (A/P) account as you did earlier in the chapter.

20 If your trial balance differs from what is in Figure 5.20, do the following:

  a. Make sure all of your changes were dated in January 2018.

  b. View the Transaction Reports you just created to locate any errors.

  c. Ask you instructor for assistance.

  d. Be sure your company matches the above as in the following chapter you'll be adding additional business events.

21 Export your Trial Balance report to Excel and save it with the file name: Student Name (replace with your name) Ch 05 Case 01 Trial Balance.xlsx.

22 Open and print the custom report you created in the last chapter called Transaction Detail by Account.

23 Export your Transactions Detail by Account report to Excel and save it with the file name: Student Name (replace with your name) Ch 05 Case 01 Transaction Detail by Account.xlsx.

24 Sign out of your company.

Case 2

Add some operating activities (purchases, credit card charges, and cash payments) to your company.

Based on what you learned in the text and using the Sample Company, you will add the following transactions to your company:

1 Add a new vendor – **E-flite**, 700 Annapolis Ln N Suite #175, Plymouth, MN, 55447, terms: net 15.

2 Add a new vendor – **Village Steak House**, 100 S El Camino Real, San Clemente, CA 92672 terms: due on receipt.

3 Add a new vendor – **Staples**, 101 Main St., San Diego, CA 92600 terms: due on receipt.

4 Add a new account – category type: **Credit Card,** detail type: **Credit Card**, name: **AMEX**

5 Add a new account – category type: **Other Current Assets**, detail type: **Other Current Assets**, name: **Supplies Asset**.

6 Add a new tracked product – name/description: **Sport Cub S**, initial quantity on hand: **0**, inventory asset account: **Inventory Asset**, price: **600.00**, cost: **479.00**, income account: **Sales**, expense account: **Cost of Goods Sold**

7 Add a new tracked product - name/description: **Mystique RES**, initial quantity on hand: **0**, inventory asset account: **Inventory Asset,** price: **450.00**, cost: **325.00**, income account: **Sales**, expense account: **Cost of Goods Sold**

8 Record a new purchase order for products on **1/2/19** – vendor: **E-flite**, product 1: **Sport Cub S**, QTY: **5**, product 2: **Mystique RES**, QTY: **3**

9   Record a new purchase order for products on **1/3/19** – vendor: **Kyosho,** product 1: **Broon F830 Ride**, QTY: **4**, product 2: **GO Aircraft Radio**, QTY: **2,** product 3: **Seawind Carbon Sailboat**, QTY: **1**

10 Record a new bill based on a purchase order #1001 on **1/7/19** – vendor: **E-flite**, terms: **Net 15**. All items ordered were received.

11 Record a new bill without a purchase order on **1/8/19** – new vendor: **San Diego News-Press**, terms: **Net 15**, account: **Advertising**, amount: **500.00**.

12 Record a new bill without a purchase order on **1/10/19** – new vendor: **Gomez Insurance**, terms: **Net 15**, account 1: **Insurance**, amount: **400.00**, account 2: **Prepaid Expenses**, amount: **4,400.00.**

13 Pay bill due to **Kyosho** on **1/18/19** using the checking account and starting with check no. 1001.

14 Record a credit card charge on **1/11/19,** vendor**: Village Steak House**, using credit card: **AMEX**, account: **Meals and Entertainment**, amount: **240.00**.

15 Record check on **1/14/19**, no.: **1002**, vendor: **Staples**, amount: **450.00**, account: **Supplies Asset**.

16 Open your previously customized report named Trial Balance 1/31/19. Your report should look like Figure 5.21.

Figure 5.21

Trial Balance (as of 1/31/19)

Case 2
TRIAL BALANCE
As of January 31, 2019

	DEBIT	CREDIT
Checking	7,150.00	
Accounts Receivable	1,425.00	
Inventory Asset	5,410.00	
Prepaid Expenses	6,800.00	
Supplies Asset	450.00	
Undeposited Funds	925.00	
Machinery & Equipment:Depreciation		1,000.00
Machinery & Equipment:Original cost	10,000.00	
Accounts Payable		8,670.00
AMEX		240.00
Notes Payable		12,000.00
Common Stock		100.00
Opening Balance Equity		0.00
Retained Earnings		8,385.00
Sales		5,700.00
Services		225.00
Cost of Goods Sold	3,020.00	
Advertising	500.00	
Insurance	400.00	
Meals and Entertainment	240.00	
TOTAL	$36,320.00	$36,320.00

17 Create and print a Transaction Report for the Checking account as you did earlier in the chapter.

18 Create and print a Transaction Report for the Inventory Asset account as you did earlier in the chapter.

19 Create and print a Transaction Report for the Accounts Payable (A/P) account as you did earlier in the chapter.

20 If your trial balance differs from what is in Figure 5.21, do the following:

    a.   Make sure that all of your changes were dated in January 2019.

    b.   View the Transaction Reports you created to locate any errors.

    c.   Ask you instructor for assistance.

    d.   Be sure your company matches the above since, in the following chapter, you will add additional business events.

21 Export your Trial Balance report to Excel and save it with the file name: Student Name (replace with your name) Ch 05 Case 02 Trial Balance.xlsx.

22 Open and print the custom report you created in the last chapter called Transaction Detail by Account.

23 Export your Transactions Detail by Account report to Excel and save it with the file name: Student Name (replace with your name) Ch 05 Case 02 Transaction Detail by Account.xlsx.

24 Sign out of your company.

Investing and Financing Activities

Student Learning Outcomes

Upon completion of this chapter, the student will be able to do the following:

- Record the acquisition of a fixed asset
- Record the acquisition of a long-term investment
- Record the sale of common stock
- Record the payment of a dividend
- Record a long-term borrowing (long-term debt)
- Record payment on long-term borrowing (long-term debt)
- Record the acquisition of a fixed asset by taking on new debt

Overview

Intuit has provided a sample company online to provide new users a test drive of its QBO product. In this chapter, you will open this sample company and practice various features of QBO. You will be recording investing activities such as acquiring a long-term investment and a fixed asset to the Sample Company file. In addition, you will be recording financing activities, such as selling common stock, paying a dividend, borrowing on a long-term basis, and making payments on long-term debt to the Sample Company file. Lastly, you will record an investing activity, acquiring a new fixed asset and a financing activity by borrowing funds to purchase the fixed asset. Remember, if you stop in the middle of this work, none of your work will be saved. So when you return, the same sample company, without your work, will appear. In some parts of the chapter, you'll be asked to sign out of the Sample Company and sign back in so the Sample Company is reset to its original state. In the end of chapter work, you will be asked to perform the same tasks completed on the Sample Company on your Student Company. That work, of course, will be saved.

Fixed Assets

In this section, you will be recording the acquisition of fixed assets. Fixed assets are long-term tangible property that a firm owns and uses in the production of its income and is not expected to be consumed or converted into cash any sooner than at least one year's time. Normally, a fixed asset's cost is depreciated over time as a means of allocating its cost over its useful life. The depreciation is recorded to a depreciation expense account and added to an accumulated depreciation (contra-asset) account. That process will be explained in the chapter on adjusting entries.

To add an asset, you will use the Check task accessed by clicking the Create (+) icon. Alternatively, you could purchase new fixed assets with using a credit card or take on new debt. The Sample Company had a fixed asset account for trucks, which you'll use to record the purchase of a truck. If you were to purchase some other type of fixed asset, equipment for example, you would need to create a new fixed asset account named Equipment and two additional sub-accounts to the Equipment account: Original Cost and Accumulated Depreciation.

To record the purchase of a new truck and new equipment in the Sample Company, do the following:

1. Open your Internet browser.

2. Type **https://qbo.intuit.com/redir/testdrive** into your browser's address text box and then press [**Enter**] to view the Sample Company Home page.

3. Click the **Create (+)** icon and then click **Check.**

4. Select + **add new** from the drop-down list in the Choose a payee text box.

5. Type **Sunset Auto** in the Name text box, select **Vendor** as the Type, and click **Save**.

6. Accept the given Payment date and Check no. provided by QBO.

7. Type **Truck:Original Cost** in the Account column of line 1

8. Type **2500.00** in the Amount column of line 1 and the press [**Tab**]. Your screen should look like Figure 6.1.

Figure 6.1

Purchase of Truck

9. Click **Save and New**.

10. Select **Tania's Nursery** from the drop-down list in the Choose a payee text box.

11. Select + **Add new** from the drop-down list in Account column of line 1.

12. Select **Fixed Assets** from the drop-down list in the Category type text box.

13 Select **Machinery & Equipment** from the drop-down list in the Detail type text box.

14 Type **Equipment** in the Name text box, and click **Save and New**.

15 Select **Fixed Assets** from the drop-down list in the Category type text box.

16 Select **Machinery & Equipment** from the drop-down list in the Detail type text box.

17 Type **Original Cost** in the Name text box.

18 Place a check in the **Is sub-account** check box.

19 Select **Equipment** from the drop-down list of accounts under the Is sub-account check box.

20 Click **Save and New**.

21 Select **Fixed Assets** from the drop-down list in the Category type text box.

22 Select **Accumulated Depreciation** from the drop-down list in the Detail type text box.

23 Type **Accumulated Depreciation** in the Name text box.

24 Place a check in the **Is sub-account** check box.

25 Select **Equipment** from the drop-down list of accounts under the Is sub-account check box.

26 Click **Save and Close**.

27 Type **Equipment:Original Cost** in the Account column of line 1.

28 Type **1000** in the Amount column of line 1 and then press [**Tab**] to see Figure 6.2.

29 Click **Save and Close**.

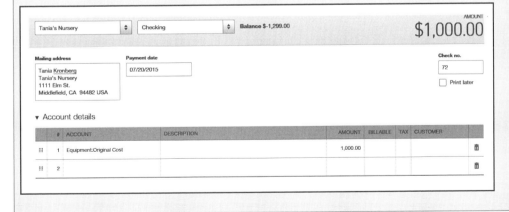

Figure 6.2

Purchase of Equipment

You have recorded the purchase of two new fixed assets.

Long-Term Investments

The acquisition of a long-term investment is another type of investing activity. In general, a long-term investment is the purchase of a financial instrument (bond, common stock, preferred stock) that matures in more than 1 year.

To record the purchase of a long-term investment in the Sample Company, do the following:

1   Continue from where you left off. If you closed the Sample Company, follow the steps to re-open it found at the beginning of this chapter.

2   Click the **Create (+)** icon, and select **Check.**

3   Select + **add new** from the drop-down list in the Choose a payee text box.

4   Type **Scottrade** in the Name text box, and select **Vendor** as the Type, and click **Save**.

5   Accept the given Payment date and Check no. provided by QBO.

6   Select + **add new** from the drop-down list in Account column of line 1.

7   Select **Other Assets** from the drop-down list in the Category Type text box.

8   Select **Other Long-term Assets** from the drop-down list in the Detail type text box.

9   Type **Investments** in the Name text box, and click **Save and Close**.

10 Type **3000** in the Amount column of line 1 and then press [**Tab**] to see Figure 6.3.

Figure 6.3

Purchase of a Long-Term Investment

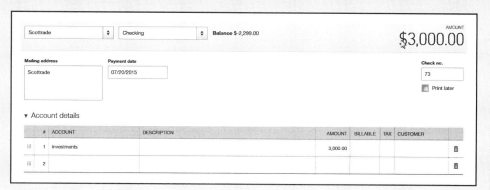

11 Click **Save and Close.**

12 Click the **Gear** icon, and click **Sign out** to reset the Sample Company.

You have recorded the purchase of a long-term investment.

Common Stock and Dividends

The sale of common stock and the payment of cash dividends to shareholders are two common financing activities. Common stock is a stockholders' equity account. Dividends are a distribution of earnings to shareholders and are accounted for as a reduction in retained earnings. Both of these are cash activities in that the sale of stock results in a cash receipt (you will account for it as a bank deposit) whereas the payment of a cash dividend results in a cash payment. There are two previous payments from customers appear when you attempt to record a bank deposit from the issuance of stock. These payments have been received but not recorded. Ignore those for now. To simplify this transaction, we will assume that the common stock is no-par common stock, and thus, no additional paid-in capital exists. Secondly we'll assume that the declaration date, record date, and payment date are all the same.

To record the sale of stock and payment of cash dividends in the Sample Company, do the following:

1   Open your Internet browser.

2   Type **https://qbo.intuit.com/redir/testdrive** into your browser's address text box, and press [**Enter**] to view the Sample Company Home page. (Do not continue from the previous work as the Sample Company file needs to be reset to its original state.)

3   Click the **Create (+)** icon and then select **Bank Deposit.**

4   Select **+ Add new** from the drop-down list in the Received From column of line 1 in the Add New Deposits section.

5   Type **WB Investments** in the Name text box, select **Vendor** in the **Type** box, and click **Save**.

6   Accept the given date provided by QBO.

7   Select **+ Add new** from the drop-down list in the Account column of line 1.

8   Select **Equity** from the drop-down list in the **Category type** text box.

9   Select **Common Stock** from the drop-down list in the **Detail type** text box.

10   Accept **Common Stock** in the **Name** text box, and click **Save and Close.**

11   Select **Check** as the Payment Method.

12   Type **10000** in the Amount column of line 1, and press [**Tab**]. Your screen should look like Figure 6.4.

Figure 6.4

Recording the Deposit of Funds from the Sale of Common Stock

13   Click **Save and Close**.

14   Click the **Create (+)** icon, and select **Check.**

15 Select + **Add new** from the drop-down list in the **Choose a payee** text box.

16 Type **Shareholders** in the Name text box, select **Vendor** in the Type box, and click **Save**.

17 Accept the given Payment date and Check no. provided by QBO.

18 Select **Retained Earnings** from the drop-down list in the Account column of line 1.

19 Type **1250** in the Amount column of line 1, and press [**Tab**]. Your screen should look like Figure 6.5.

Figure 6.5

Payment of Dividends

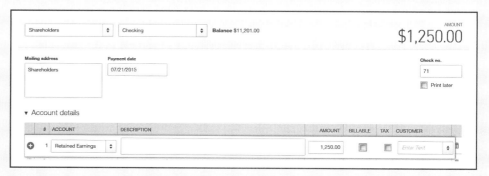

20 Click **Save and Close**.

21 Do not sign out of the Sample Company.

Long-Term Debt

The borrowing of funds on a long-term basis and the repayment of debt are two additional financing activities. Both of these are cash activities in that the borrowing of funds results in a cash receipt (you will account for it as a bank deposit) whereas the payment of the debt results in a cash payment. There are two previous payments from customers that appear when you attempt to record a bank deposit from the borrowing of funds. These payments have been received but not recorded. You'll ignore those for now. This company decided to take the funds from the stock sale recorded above and the new borrowings below to pay off the old long-term debt with interest.

To record the receipt of funds from borrowing and the payment of long-term debt in the Sample Company, do the following:

1 Continue from where you left off. If you closed the Sample Company, follow the steps to re-open it found at the beginning of this chapter.

2 Click the **Create (+)** icon and then select **Bank Deposit.**

3 Select + **Add new** from the drop-down list in the Received From column of line 1 in the Add New Deposits section.

4 Type **Bank of La Jolla** in the Name text box, select **Vendor** in the Type box, and click **Save**.

5   Accept the given date provided by QBO.

6   Select **Notes Payable** from the drop-down list in Account column of line 1.

7   Select **Check** from the drop-down list in the Payment Method column of line 1.

8   Type **15000** in the Amount column of line 1, and press [**Tab**]. Your screen should look like Figure 6.6.

Figure 6.6

Recording the Deposit of Funds from Borrowing

9   Click **Save and Close.**

10 Click the **Create (+)** icon, and select **Check.**

11 Select + **Add new** from the drop-down list in the Choose a payee text box.

12 Type **Bank of San Diego** in the Name text box, select **Vendor** in the Type box, and click **Save.**

13 Accept the given Payment date and Check no. provided by QBO.

14 Select **Notes Payable** from the drop-down list in the Account column of line 1.

15 Type **25000** in the Amount column of line 1 and then press [**Tab**].

16 Select + **Add new** from the drop-down list in the Account column of line 2.

17 Select **Expenses** from the drop-down list in the Category Type text box.

18 Select **Interest Paid** from the drop-down list in the Detail Type text box.

19 Type **Interest Expense** in the Name text box and click **Save and Close.**

20 Type **1000** in the Amount column of line 2, and press [**Tab**] Your screen should look like Figure 6.7.

Figure 6.7

Repayment of Long-Term Debt
with Interest

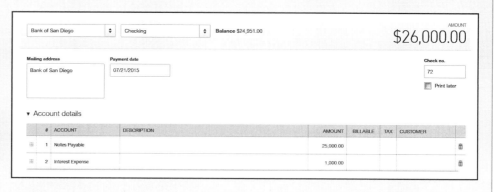

21 Click **Save and Close**.

22 Do not sign out of the Sample Company.

Acquisition of a Fixed Asset in Exchange for Long-Term Debt

You completed the process for recording an investing activity (purchase of a fixed asset) and a financing activity (borrowing on a long-term basis). Both of these transactions were recorded by affecting the checking account (cash).

Occasionally, a company acquires a fixed asset by issuing long-term debt, for example, purchasing another truck in exchange for a note payable. This cannot be recorded using the checking account since no funds were exchanged. Instead, you will use the journal entry process to record the fixed asset acquisition and the long-term debt borrowing.

To record the purchase of a fixed asset by issuing debt, do the following:

1 Continue from where you left off. If you closed the Sample Company, follow the steps to re-open it found at the beginning of this chapter.

2 Click the **Create (+)** icon, and select **Journal Entry.**

3 Accept the Journal date and Journal no. provided by QBO.

4 Select **Truck: Original Cost** from the drop-down list in the Account column of line 1.

5 Type **3400** in the Debits column of line 1.

6 Select **Notes Payable** from the drop-down list in the Account column of line 2.

7 Accept **3400** in the Credits column of line 2, and press [**Tab**] to view the journal entry shown in Figure 6.8.

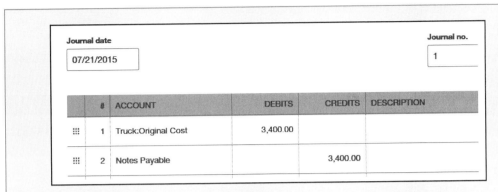

Figure 6.8

Journal Entry to Record Purchase of Fixed Asset in Exchange for Long-Term Debt

8 Click **Save and Close**.

9 Sign out of the Sample Company.

End Note

In this chapter, you recorded investing activities: the acquisition of fixed assets and of long-term investments, the sale of common stocks, the payment of a dividend, the borrowing and payment of long-term debt, and the acquisition of fixed assets by taking on new debt. In the next chapter, you will work with payroll.

Chapter 6 Questions

1 What are the steps to record the acquisition of a fixed asset using a check?

2 What are the steps to record the acquisition of a fixed asset for a note payable?

3 What are the steps to record the sale of common stock?

4 What are the steps to record the payment of dividends?

5 What are the steps to record borrowing on a note payable?

Chapter 6 Matching

a. Operating activity

b. Investing activity

c. Financing activity

d. Fixed assets

e. Long-term investment

f. Common stock

g. Dividends

h. Long-term debt

i. Bank deposit

j. Journal entry

_____ Long-term tangible property that a firm owns

_____ Distribution of earnings to shareholders

_____ A stockholders' equity account

_____ Used to record purchase of a fixed asset for a note

_____ A-5 year note payable

_____ Sales receipt

_____ A financial instrument that matures in more than 1 year

_____ Used to record amounts received from a note payable

_____ Sale of common stock

_____ Purchase of common stock

Chapter 6 Cases

The following cases require you to open the company you updated in Chapter 5. Each case below is continued throughout the text in a sequential manner. For example, if you are assigned Case 1, you will use the file you modified in this chapter in all following chapters. Each case below is similar in concepts assessed but differs in amounts and transactions.

To reopen your company, do the following:

1 Open your Internet browser.

2 Type **https://qbo.intuit.com/qbo28/login?webredir** into your browser's address text box.

3 Type your User ID and Password into the text boxes as you have done before.

Case 1

Now add some investing and financing activities to your company.

Based on what you learned in the text and using the Sample Company, you are to add the following transactions to your company:

1 Create three new fixed asset accounts: category type: **Fixed Asset**, detail type: **Machinery & Equipment** and **Accumulated Depreciation** (where appropriate), account names: **Equipment**, **Original Cost** (a sub account of Equipment), and **Accumulated Depreciation** (a sub account of Equipment).

2 Create a new asset account with a category type: **Other Assets**, detail type: **Other Long-term Assets**, name: **Investments**.

3 Record the purchase of a new computer on **1/10/18** from **Office Depot**, check: **1003**, amount: **$1,375.00**, account: **Equipment:Original Cost**.

4 Record a long-term investment on **1/11/18** to **Etrade** (a new vendor), check **1004**, amount: **$4,000**, account: **Investments**.

5 Record the sale of common stock on **1/12/18** to **Shareholders** (a new vendor), deposit amount: **$20,000**, account: **Common Stock**.

6 Record the payment of dividends to **Shareholders** on **1/15/18**, check **1005**, in the amount of **$500**.

7 Record the deposit of funds from a new note payable signed on **1/16/18** with **Bank of CA** (a new vendor) in the amount of **$65,000**.

8 Record the payment to **Rabo Bank** (a new vendor) to retire an existing note payable on **1/16/18** of **$60,000** with interest of **$600** using check **1006**.

9 Record the purchase of an additional computer on **1/17/18** from **Office Depot** in exchange for a note payable of **$1,800**.

10 Open your previously customized report named Trial Balance 1/31/18. Your report should look like Figure 6.9.

11 Create and print a Transaction Report for the Checking account.

12 Create and print a Transaction Report for the Equipment:Original Cost account.

13 Create and print a Transaction Report for the Notes Payable account.

14 Create and print a Transaction Report for the Common Stock account.

15 If your trial balance differs from Figure 6.9, do the following:

   a. Make sure that all of your changes were dated in January 2018.

   b. View the Transaction Reports you just created to locate any errors.

   c. Ask you instructor for assistance.

   d. Be sure your company matches the above as in the following chapter you'll be adding additional business events.

Figure 6.9

Trial Balance as of 1/31/18

Case 1
TRIAL BALANCE
As of January 31, 2018

	DEBIT	CREDIT
Checking	34,850.00	
Accounts Receivable	1,030.00	
Inventory Asset	11,800.00	
Prepaid Expenses	8,000.00	
Supplies Asset	375.00	
Undeposited Funds	5,000.00	
Equipment:Original Cost	3,175.00	
Furniture & Fixtures:Depreciation		10,000.00
Furniture & Fixtures:Original cost	40,000.00	
Investments	4,000.00	
Accounts Payable		7,645.00
VISA		1,800.00
Notes Payable		66,800.00
Common Stock		21,000.00
Opening Balance Equity		0.00
Retained Earnings		5,000.00
Sales		2,160.00
Services		170.00
Cost of Goods Sold	1,300.00	
Interest Expense	600.00	
Rent or Lease	2,500.00	
Travel	1,800.00	
Utilities	145.00	
TOTAL	$114,575.00	$114,575.00

16 Export your Trial Balance report to Excel, and save it with the file name: Student Name (replace with your name) Ch 06 Case 01 Trial Balance.xlsx.

17 Open and print the custom report you created in the last chapter called Transaction Detail by Account.

18 Export your Transactions Detail by Account report to Excel, and save it with the file name: Student Name (replace with your name) Ch 06 Case 01 Transaction Detail by Account.xlsx.

19 Sign out of your company.

Case 2

Now add some investing and financing activities to your company.

Based on what you learned in the text and using the Sample Company, you are to add the following transactions to your company:

1 Create three new fixed asset accounts: category type: **Fixed Asset**, detail type: **Furniture & Fixtures** and **Accumulated Depreciation** (where appropriate), account names: **Furniture**, **Original Cost** (a sub account of **Furniture**), and **Accumulated Depreciation** (a sub account of **Furniture**).

2 Create a new asset account with a category type: **Other Assets**, detail type: **Other Long-term Assets**, name: **Investments**.

3 Record the purchase of new furniture on **1/11/19** from **Staples**, check: **1003**, amount: **$2,250.00,** account**: Furniture:Original Cost**.

4 Record a long-term investment on **1/11/19** to **Raymond James** (a new vendor), check **1004**, amount: **$3,200**, account: **Investments**.

5 Record the sale of common stock on **1/14/19** to **Shareholders** (a new vendor), deposit amount: **$25,000**, account: **Common Stock**.

6 Record the payment of dividends to **Shareholders** on **1/15/19**, check **1005**, in the amount of **$800**.

7 Record the deposit of funds from a new note payable signed on **1/16/19** with **Bank of TJ** (a new vendor) in the amount of $**25,000**.

8 Record the payment to **Community Bank** (a new vendor) to retire an existing note payable on **1/16/19** of **$12,000** with interest of **$300** using check **1006**.

9 Record the purchase of additional furniture from **Staples** on **1/17/19** in exchange for a note payable of **$2,625**.

10 Open your previously customized report named Trial Balance 1/31/19. Your report should look like Figure 6.10.

Figure 6.10

Trial Balance as of 1/31/19

Case 2
TRIAL BALANCE
As of January 31, 2019

	DEBIT	CREDIT
Checking	38,600.00	
Accounts Receivable	1,425.00	
Inventory Asset	5,410.00	
Prepaid Expenses	6,800.00	
Supplies Asset	450.00	
Undeposited Funds	925.00	
Furniture:Original Cost	4,875.00	
Machinery & Equipment:Depreciation		1,000.00
Machinery & Equipment:Original cost	10,000.00	
Investments	3,200.00	
Accounts Payable		8,670.00
AMEX		240.00
Notes Payable		27,625.00
Common Stock		25,100.00
Opening Balance Equity		0.00
Retained Earnings		7,585.00
Sales		5,700.00
Services		225.00
Cost of Goods Sold	3,020.00	
Advertising	500.00	
Insurance	400.00	
Interest Expense	300.00	
Meals and Entertainment	240.00	
TOTAL	$76,145.00	$76,145.00

11   Create and print a Transaction Report for the Checking account.

12   Create and print a Transaction Report for the Furniture:Original Cost account.

13   Create and print a Transaction Report for the Notes Payable account.

14   Create and print a Transaction Report for the Common Stock account.

15   If your trial balance differs from Figure 6.10, do the following:

   a.   Make sure that all of your changes were dated in January 2019.

   b.   View the Transaction Reports you created to locate any errors.

   c.   Ask you instructor for assistance.

   d.   Be sure your company matches the above, because in the following chapter, you will be adding additional business events.

16   Export your Trial Balance report to Excel, and save it with the file name: Student Name (replace with your name) Ch 06 Case 02 Trial Balance.xlsx.

17   Open and print the custom report you created in the last chapter called Transaction Detail by Account.

18   Export your Transactions Detail by Account report to Excel, and save it with the file name: Student Name (replace with your name) Ch 06 Case 02 Transaction Detail by Account.xlsx.

19   Sign out of your company.

Payroll

Overview

Intuit has provided a Sample Company online to let new users test drive its QBO product. In this chapter, you will open this Sample Company and practice payroll activities in QBO. QBO Payroll is an add-on feature to QBO. You can use a trial version of QBO Payroll, but it only lasts for 30 days. Even though the payroll features available through QBO Payroll are extensive and helpful, they focus on real companies and real time frames. Thus, this chapter will focus on the creation of new employees, general ledger accounts, and payment to employees without the use of QBO Payroll.

Remember, if you stop in the middle of this work, none of your work will be saved. So, when you return, the same sample company, without your work, will appear. In some parts of the chapter, you will be asked to sign out of the Sample Company and sign back in so the Sample Company is reset to its original state. In the end of chapter work, you will be asked to perform the same tasks completed on the Sample Company on your Student Company. That work, of course, will be saved.

Employees

In this section, you will be adding a new employee to QBO.

To add a new employee to the Sample Company, do the following:

1. Open your Internet browser.

2. Type **https://qbo.intuit.com/redir/testdrive** into your browser's address text box, and press [**Enter**] to view the Sample Company Home page.

3 Click the **Employees** menu in the navigation bar.

4 Click the **Add Employee** button.

5 Click the **Not right now** button when asked to Turn payroll on.

6 Type **Mae West** as the employee's name and provide the following address information: **2393 Ridge Place #3, Rancho Mar, CA, 93154**. Type **322-31-8999** as the employee's social security number (SSN). Your screen should look like Figure 7.1.

Figure 7.1

Employee Information (adding a new employee)

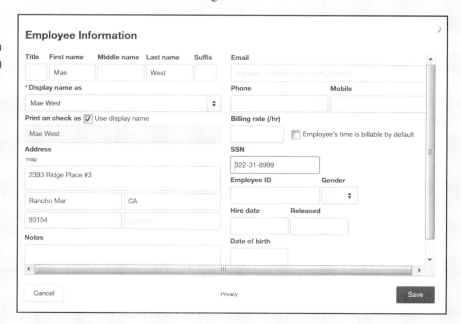

7 Click **Save**.

8 Your Employee window should now reflect three employees shown in Figure 7.2.

Figure 7.2

Employees

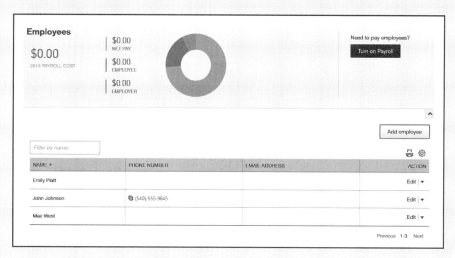

Payroll Accounts

Once again, if you were using QuickBooks Payroll Online, general ledger accounts to capture payroll information would be created for you in the setup process. However, since you are not using QuickBooks Payroll Online, you will have to create them on your own. To keep things simple, you can create the minimum two new accounts for payroll: Payroll (expense) and Payroll Tax Payable (liability).

An employer agrees to pay its employees a salary per month or an hourly rate. In either case, for the agreed upon salary or hourly rate times hours worked, amounts are recorded to the Payroll (expense) account. Depending on the state, employees are often required to have an estimated amount of federal and state income taxes withheld from their paychecks by their employers. In addition, employers must withhold social security (6.2%) and Medicare (1.45%) taxes. Amounts withheld from employees will be recorded in the Payroll Tax Payable (liability) account until remitted to the U.S. Treasury and state government entities. Employers must match those amounts for social security (6.2%) and Medicare (1.45%) taxes. These matching costs will be recorded as additional Payroll (expense).

To add payroll related accounts to the Sample Company, do the following:

1   Continue from where you left off. If you closed the Sample Company, follow the steps to re-open it found at the beginning of this chapter.

2   Click the **Gear** icon and then click **Chart of Accounts.**

3   Click New

4   Select **Expenses** from the drop-down list in the **Category Type** text box.

5   Select **Payroll Expenses** from the drop-down list in the **Detail Type** text box.

6   Type **Payroll** in the Name text box replacing Payroll Expenses as shown in Figure 7.3.

Figure 7.3

Account (adding a new payroll account)

7 Click **Save and New.**

8 Select **Other Current Liabilities** from the drop-down list in the **Category Type** text box.

9 Select **Payroll Tax Payable** from the drop-down list in the **Detail Type** text box.

10 Type **Payroll Tax Payable** in the **Name** text box.

11 Click **Save and Close.**

12 Do not sign out of the Sample Company.

You have added two payroll-related general ledger accounts.

Pay Employees

The payment of employees requires gathering information from each employee that helps determine withholding amounts and payroll expenses. The federal and state governments provide formulas and/or tables to help employers calculate these amounts. In this text, you will be provided these amounts. Additional taxes such as training, unemployment, etc., are ignored for this illustration. Since payroll is a recurring event, it will help to make these checks recur, which can be edited each payroll for changes in hours worked where applicable. In this example payroll is paid semi-monthly.

See Figure 7.4 for a payroll for your Sample Company:

Figure 7.4

Semi-Monthly Payroll Information

Pay/Tax/Withholding	Emily	John	Mae	Total
Hours if applicable	n/a	80	60	
Annual salary or hourly rate	$ 60,000	$ 18.00	$ 18.00	
Gross pay	**2,500.00**	**1,440.00**	**1,080.00**	**5,020.00**
Federal withholding	342.50	197.28	147.96	**687.74**
Social security employee (6.2%)	155.00	89.28	66.96	**311.24**
Medicare employee (1.45%)	36.25	20.88	15.66	**72.79**
Employee withholding	**533.75**	**307.44**	**230.58**	**1,071.77**
Social security employer (6.2%)	155.00	89.28	66.96	**311.24**
Medicare company employer (1.45%)	36.25	20.88	15.66	**72.79**
Employer payroll tax expense	**191.25**	**110.16**	**82.62**	**384.03**
Net Check amount	1,966.25	1,132.56	849.42	**3,948.23**

To record the payment of employees in the Sample Company, do the following:

1   Continue from where you left off.

2   Click the **Create (+)** icon, and select **Check.**

3   Select **Emily Platt** from the drop-down list (note: employees are located at the bottom of the list.) in the **Choose a payee** text box.

4   Accept the given date and check number QBO provides.

5   Select **Payroll** from the drop-down list in Account column of line 1.

6   Type **2500** in the Amount column of line 1 and press **[Tab]** 4 times.

7   Select **Payroll Tax Payable** from the drop-down list in Account column of line 2.

8   Type **−533.75** in the Amount column of line 1 and press **[Tab]** 4 times. (Be sure to enter this amount as a negative number.)

9   Select **Payroll** from the drop-down list in Account column of line 3.

10   Type **191.25** in the Amount column of line 3 and press **[Tab]** 4 times.

11   Select **Payroll Tax Payable** from the drop-down list in Account column of line 2.

12   Type **−191.25** in the Amount column of line 4 and press **[Tab]** 4 times. (Be sure to enter this amount as a negative number.) Your screen should look like Figure 7.5.

Figure 7.5

Check #71 (paycheck for Emily Platt)

13   Click **Make Recurring** located at the bottom of the screen.

14   Select **Unscheduled** from the drop-down list in the **Type** text box.

15   Click **Save template**.

16   Click the **Gear** icon.

17   Select **Recurring Transactions** located in the List column.

18   Click **Use** located in the Action column. The check window will appear again completed like that shown in Figure 7.5.

19 Make sure the date is correct and then click **Save and New**.

20 Enter payroll information found in Figure 7.4 for John and Mae in the same way as you entered payroll information for Emily above. Be sure to make each of these unscheduled recurring events.

21 After entering the last check to record payroll above, click **Save and Close**.

22 Click **Reports** from the navigation bar.

23 Type **Trial Balance** in the Go to report search box and then press [**Enter**] to view a current trial balance, the top of which is shown in Figure 7.6.

Figure 7.6

Trial Balance (partial view)

Craig's Design and Landscaping Services
TRIAL BALANCE
As of July 22, 2015

	DEBIT	CREDIT
Checking		2,747.23
Savings	800.00	
Accounts Receivable (A/R)	5,281.52	
Inventory Asset	596.25	
Undeposited Funds	2,062.52	
Truck:Original Cost	13,495.00	
Accounts Payable (A/P)		1,602.67
Mastercard		157.72
Arizona Dept. of Revenue Payable		0.00
Board of Equalization Payable		370.94
Loan Payable		4,000.00
Payroll Tax Payable		1,455.80
Notes Payable		25,000.00
Opening Balance Equity	9,337.50	

24 Click the **2,747.23** amount on the Checking line to view a transaction report for the checking account shown in Figure 7.7.

Figure 7.7

Transaction Report (checking account)

Craig's Design and Landscaping Services
TRANSACTION REPORT
July 1-22, 2015

DATE	TRANSACTION TYPE	NUM	NAME	MEMO/DESCRIPTION	ACCOUNT	SPLIT	AMOUNT	BALANCE
Checking								
Beginning Balance								2,101.00
07/10/2015	Credit Card Credit				Checking	Mastercard	-900.00	1,201.00
07/22/2015	Check	71	Emily Platt		Checking	-Split-	-1,966.25	-765.25
07/22/2015	Check	73	Mae West		Checking	-Split-	-849.42	-1,614.67
07/22/2015	Check	72	John Johnson		Checking	-Split-	-1,132.56	-2,747.23
Total for Checking							$ -4,848.23	
TOTAL							$ -4,848.23	

25 Match your screen with Figure 7.7, which may be in a different order than yours. (It shows different dates.)

26 Click **John Johnson** to view the payroll check shown in Figure 7.8.

Figure 7.8

Check #72 (John Johnson payroll check)

27 Match your screen to Figure 7.8, and close the check window.

28 Click **Back to Summary Report** to return to the Trial Balance report.

You have recorded payroll for one semi-monthly period. You can practice with another payroll using the recurring transactions you have set up.

29 Click the **Gear** icon, and click **Recurring transactions** located in the Lists column to view a list of recurring transactions shown in Figure 7.9. (If your list does not contain the three employees you recorded, you will need to return to these transactions, and click the Make recurring button.)

Figure 7.9

Recurring Transactions

30 Click **Use** on the Mae West template to view a new payroll check for Mae.

31 Add 14 days to the **Payment date** text box representing the next semi-monthly period. In this example, the new date is 8/6/2015; of course, yours will differ.

32 Payroll information for this next semi-monthly period is shown in Figure 7.10. Note the hours worked are different and John received an increase in his hourly rate.

Figure 7.10

Semi-Monthly
Payroll Information

Pay/Tax/Withholding	Emily	John	Mae	Total
Hours if applicable	n/a	75	63	
Annual salary or hourly rate	$ 60,000	$ 20.00	$ 18.00	
Gross pay	**2,500.00**	**1,500.00**	**1,134.00**	**5,134.00**
Federal withholding	342.50	205.50	155.36	**703.36**
Social security employee (6.2%)	155.00	93.00	70.31	**318.31**
Medicare employee (1.45%)	36.25	21.75	16.44	**74.44**
Employee withholding	**533.75**	**320.25**	**242.11**	1,096.11
Social security employer (6.2%)	155.00	93.00	70.31	**318.31**
Medicare company employer (1.45%)	36.25	21.75	16.44	**74.44**
Employer payroll tax expense	**191.25**	**114.75**	**86.75**	**392.75**
Net Check amount	1,966.25	1,179.75	891.89	**4,037.89**

33 Type **1134** in the Amount column on line 1.

34 Type **-242.11** in the Amount column on line 2.

35 Type **86.75** in the Amount column on line 3.

36 Type **-86.75** in the Amount column on line 4. Your screen should now look like Figure 7.11.

Figure 7.11

Check #74 (Mae West payroll check)

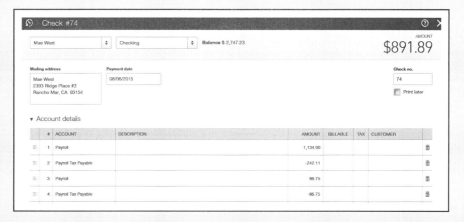

37 Click **Save and close**.

38 Use the same process (clicking **Use** from the Recurring Transactions list) for John and Emily to record their paychecks based on the new information shown in Figure 7.10. (Since Emily is salaried, her information remains the same each pay period, so nothing needs to be changed from the recurring transaction information provided.) Click **Yes** to accept a duplicate check number if QBO identifies that the check number you are proposing has been used.

39 Click **Reports** from the navigation bar.

40 Type **Trial Balance** in the Go to report search box, and press [**Enter**].

41 Change the To: date in the report to include whatever date you used to enter the most recent semi-monthly payroll. In our example, that date was 8/6/15. Your date will differ. When changed, click Run report to see a partial view of the trial balance shown in Figure 7.12.

Craig's Design and Landscaping Services
TRIAL BALANCE
As of August 6, 2015

	DEBIT	CREDIT
Checking		6,785.12
Savings	800.00	
Accounts Receivable (A/R)	5,281.52	
Inventory Asset	596.25	
Undeposited Funds	2,062.52	
Truck:Original Cost	13,495.00	
Accounts Payable (A/P)		1,602.67
Mastercard		157.72
Arizona Dept. of Revenue Payable		0.00
Board of Equalization Payable		370.94
Loan Payable		4,000.00
Payroll Tax Payable		2,944.66
Notes Payable		25,000.00
Opening Balance Equity	9,337.50	

Figure 7.12

Trial Balance (partial view)

42 Click the **6,785.12** amount on the Checking line to view a transaction report for the checking account shown in Figure 7.13.

Craig's Design and Landscaping Services
TRANSACTION REPORT
July 1 - August 6, 2015

DATE	TRANSACTION TYPE	NUM	NAME	MEMO/DESCRIPTION	ACCOUNT	SPLIT	AMOUNT	BALANCE
Checking								
Beginning Balance								2,101.00
07/10/2015	Credit Card Credit				Checking	Mastercard	-900.00	1,201.00
07/22/2015	Check	73	Mae West		Checking	-Split-	-849.42	351.58
07/22/2015	Check	71	Emily Platt		Checking	-Split-	-1,966.25	-1,614.67
07/22/2015	Check	72	John Johnson		Checking	-Split-	-1,132.56	-2,747.23
08/06/2015	Check	76	Emily Platt		Checking	-Split-	-1,966.25	-4,713.48
08/06/2015	Check	74	Mae West		Checking	-Split-	-891.89	-5,605.37
08/06/2015	Check	75	John Johnson		Checking	-Split-	-1,179.75	-6,785.12
Total for Checking							$ -8,886.12	
TOTAL							$ -8,886.12	

Figure 7.13

Transaction Report (checking account)

43 Match your screen with Figure 7.13, which may be in a different order than yours. It will show different dates. Take note of any differences.

44 Click any payroll-related transaction if you want to drill down to the payroll check you recorded to see if you can fix any differences noted.

45 Fix any errors you discover.

46 Sign out of this Sample Company.

You have recorded two semi-monthly payroll checks for the Sample Company. Keep in mind that since you are not using QuickBooks Payroll Online, there are no employee records of earnings or taxes.

End Note

In this chapter, you added a new employee, a new payroll (expense) account, and a new payroll tax payable (liability) account and paid employees. In the next chapter, you will work with budgets and bank reconciliations.

Chapter 7 Questions

1   What are the steps to create a new employee?

2   What are the steps to create a new account?

3   What are the two minimum accounts needed to account for payroll?

4   What types of costs are included in the Payroll (expense) account?

5   What types of costs are included in the Payroll Tax Payable (liability) account?

Chapter 7 Matching

a. 6.2%

b. 1.45%

c. Payroll

d. Payroll tax payable

e. QBO Payroll

f. Gross pay

g. Recurring transactions

h. Transaction report

i. Unscheduled

j. Record as negative amounts

_____ Account used to record the liability for Federal income tax withheld

_____ An Add-on feature to QBO

_____ Rate used to calculate an employee's Medicare tax

_____ Hours worked times hourly rate

_____ Use to more efficiently record periodic payroll

_____ Payroll tax payable

_____ Accessed by clicking an amount on the trial balance

_____ One type of recurring event

_____ Account used to record all payroll expenses

_____ Rate used to calculate an employee's social security tax

Chapter 7 Cases

The following cases require you to open the company you updated in Chapter 6. Each case below continues throughout the text in a sequential manner. For example, if you are assigned Case 1, you will use the file you modified in this chapter in all following chapters. Each case below is similar in concepts assessed but differs in amounts and transactions.

To reopen your company, do the following:

1   Open your Internet browser.

2   Type **https://qbo.intuit.com/qbo28/login?webredir** into your browser's address text box.

3   Type your User ID and Password into the text boxes as you have done before.

Case 1

Do not install QBO Payroll. Based on what you learned in the text and using the Sample Company, you are to add the following payroll-related activities to your company:

1 Add two new accounts like you did in the chapter: Payroll (expense) and Payroll Tax Payable (liability).

2 Add a new employee: Ben Franklin, 32 Ocean View Lane, La Jolla, CA, 92037, social security number: 556-12-3467.

3 Add a second employee: Betsy Ross, 2323 1st Street, La Jolla, CA, 92037, social security number: 458-87-1974.

4 Payroll is paid twice a month on the 17th and the last day of each month.

5 Record payroll (as you did in the chapter) for 1/17/18 based on the information shown in Figure 7.14. After recording each employee's check, be sure to designate it as a recurring transaction.

Pay/Tax/Withholding	Ben	Betsy	Total
Hours if applicable	n/a	73	
Annual salary or hourly rate	$ 95,000	$ 21.50	
Gross pay	**3,958.33**	**1,569.50**	**5,527.83**
Federal withholding	542.29	215.02	**757.31**
Social security employee (6.2%)	245.42	97.31	**342.73**
Medicare employee (1.45%)	57.40	22.76	**80.16**
Employee withholding	**845.11**	**335.09**	**1,180.20**
Social security employer (6.2%)	245.42	97.31	**342.73**
Medicare company employer (1.45%)	57.40	22.76	**80.16**
Employer payroll tax expense	**302.82**	**120.07**	**422.89**
Net Check amount	3,113.22	1,234.41	**4,347.63**

Figure 7.14

Payroll information (for 1/17/18)

6 Use the recurring transactions template you created above to help you record payroll (as you did in the chapter) for 1/31/18 based on the information shown in Figure 7.15.

Figure 7.15

Payroll information (for 1/31/18)

Pay/Tax/Withholding	Ben	Betsy	Total
Hours if applicable	n/a	68	
Annual salary or hourly rate	$ 95,000	$ 21.50	
Gross pay	3,958.33	1,462.00	5,420.33
Federal withholding	542.29	200.29	742.58
Social security employee (6.2%)	245.42	90.64	336.06
Medicare employee (1.45%)	57.40	21.20	78.60
Employee withholding	845.11	312.13	1,157.24
Social security employer (6.2%)	245.42	90.64	336.06
Medicare company employer (1.45%)	57.40	21.20	78.60
Employer payroll tax expense	302.82	111.84	414.66
Net Check amount	3,113.22	1,149.87	4,263.09

7 Open your previously customized report named Trial Balance 1/31/18. Your report should look like Figure 7.16.

Figure 7.16

Trial Balance (as of 1/31/18)

	DEBIT	CREDIT
Checking	26,239.28	
Accounts Receivable	1,030.00	
Inventory Asset	11,800.00	
Prepaid Expenses	8,000.00	
Supplies Asset	375.00	
Undeposited Funds	5,000.00	
Equipment:Original Cost	3,175.00	
Furniture & Fixtures:Depreciation		10,000.00
Furniture & Fixtures:Original cost	40,000.00	
Investments	4,000.00	
Accounts Payable		7,645.00
Visa		1,800.00
Payroll Tax Payable		3,174.99
Notes Payable		66,800.00
Common Stock		21,000.00
Opening Balance Equity		0.00
Retained Earnings		5,000.00
Sales		2,160.00
Services		170.00
Cost of Goods Sold	1,300.00	
Interest Expense	600.00	
Payroll	11,785.71	
Rent or Lease	2,500.00	
Travel	1,800.00	
Utilities	145.00	
TOTAL	$117,749.99	$117,749.99

8   Create and print a Transaction Report for the Checking account.

9   Create and print a Transaction Report for the Payroll Tax Payable account.

10 If your trial balance differs from the one in Figure 7.16, do the following:

    a.   Make sure all of your changes were dated in January 2018.

    b.   View the Transaction Reports you created to locate any errors.

    c.   Ask you instructor for assistance.

    d.   Be sure your company matches the above since, in the following chapter, you will add additional business events.

11 Export your Trial Balance report to Excel, and save it with the file name: Student Name (replace with your name) Ch 07 Case 01 Trial Balance.xlsx.

12 Open and print the custom report you created in the last chapter called Transaction Detail by Account.

13 Export your Transactions Detail by Account report to Excel, and save it with the file name: Student Name (replace with your name) Ch 07 Case 01 Transaction Detail by Account.xlsx.

14 Sign out of your company.

Case 2

Do not install QBO Payroll. Based on what you learned in the text and using the Sample Company, you are to add the following payroll-related activities to your company:

1   Add two new accounts like you did in the chapter: Payroll (expense) and Payroll Tax Payable (liability).

2   Add a new employee: Frank Benjamin, 32 Ocean View Lane, La Jolla, CA, 92037, social security number: 556-12-3467

3   Add a second employee: Sara Juarez, 2323 1st Street, La Jolla, CA, 92037, social security number: 458-87-1974.

4   Payroll is paid twice a month on the 16th and the last day of each month.

5   Record payroll (like you did in the chapter) for 1/16/19 based on the information shown in Figure 7.17. After recording each employee's check, be sure to designate it as a recurring transaction.

Figure 7.17

Payroll information (for 1/16/19)

Pay/Tax/Withholding	Frank	Sara	Total
Hours if applicable	n/a	71	
Annual salary or hourly rate	$ 72,000	$ 18.75	
Gross pay	**3,000.00**	**1,331.25**	**4,331.25**
Federal withholding	411.00	182.38	**593.38**
Social security employee (6.2%)	186.00	82.54	**268.54**
Medicare employee (1.45%)	43.50	19.30	**62.80**
Employee withholding	**640.50**	**284.22**	**924.72**
Social security employer (6.2%)	186.00	82.54	**268.54**
Medicare company employer (1.45%)	43.50	19.30	**62.80**
Employer payroll tax expense	**229.50**	**101.84**	**331.34**
Net Check amount	2,359.50	1,047.03	**3,406.53**

6 Use the recurring transactions template you created above to help you record payroll (as you did in the chapter) for 1/31/19 based on the information shown in Figure 7.18.

Figure 7.18

Payroll Information (for 1/31/19)

Pay/Tax/Withholding	Frank	Sara	Total
Hours if applicable	n/a	66	
Annual salary or hourly rate	$ 72,000	$ 18.75	
Gross pay	**3,000.00**	**1,237.50**	**4,237.50**
Federal withholding	411.00	169.54	**580.54**
Social security employee (6.2%)	186.00	76.73	**262.73**
Medicare employee (1.45%)	43.50	17.94	**61.44**
Employee withholding	**640.50**	**264.21**	**904.71**
Social security employer (6.2%)	186.00	76.73	**262.73**
Medicare company employer (1.45%)	43.50	17.94	**61.44**
Employer payroll tax expense	**229.50**	**94.67**	**324.17**
Net Check amount	2,359.50	973.29	**3,332.79**

7 Open your previously customized report named Trial Balance 1/31/19. Your report should look like Figure 7.19.

Figure 7.19

Trial Balance (as of 1/31/19)

Case 2
TRIAL BALANCE
As of January 31, 2019

	DEBIT	CREDIT
Checking	31,860.68	
Accounts Receivable	1,425.00	
Inventory Asset	5,410.00	
Prepaid Expenses	6,800.00	
Supplies Asset	450.00	
Undeposited Funds	925.00	
Furniture:Original Cost	4,875.00	
Machinery & Equipment:Depreciation		1,000.00
Machinery & Equipment:Original cost	10,000.00	
Investments	3,200.00	
Accounts Payable		8,670.00
AMEX		240.00
Payroll Tax Payable		2,484.94
Notes Payable		27,625.00
Common Stock		25,100.00
Opening Balance Equity		0.00
Retained Earnings		7,585.00
Sales		5,700.00
Services		225.00
Cost of Goods Sold	3,020.00	
Advertising	500.00	
Insurance	400.00	
Interest Expense	300.00	
Meals and Entertainment	240.00	
Payroll	9,224.26	
TOTAL	$78,629.94	$78,629.94

8   Create and print a Transaction Report for the Checking account.

9   Create and print a Transaction Report for the Payroll Tax Payable account.

10   If your trial balance differs from the one in Figure 7.19, do the following:

   a.   Make sure all of your changes were dated in January 2019.

   b.   View the Transaction Reports you created to locate any errors.

   c.   Ask you instructor for assistance.

   d.   Be sure your company matches the above since, in the following chapter, you will add additional business events.

11   Export your Trial Balance report to Excel, and save it with the file name: Student Name (replace with your name) Ch 07 Case 02 Trial Balance.xlsx.

12   Open and print the custom report you created in the last chapter called Transaction Detail by Account.

13   Export your Transactions Detail by Account report to Excel, and save it with the file name: Student Name (replace with your name) Ch 07 Case 02 Transaction Detail by Account.xlsx.

14   Sign out of your company.

Budgets and Bank Reconciliations

Student Learning Outcomes

Upon completion of this chapter, the student will be able to do the following:

- Add budget amounts to create a budget
- Create Profit and Loss budget reports
- Reconcile a checking account and print a reconciliation report

Overview

Intuit has provided a sample company online to provide new users a test drive of its QBO product. In this chapter, you will open this sample company and practice budget activities in QBO and reconcile a bank account. Budgets and bank reconciliations provide internal control over business activities. Significant deviations between actual and budget amounts could identify and help resolve problems. Unexplained differences identified in bank reconciliations can point to possible fraud or incompetency issues.

Remember, if you stop in the middle of this work none of your work will be saved. So, when you return, the same sample company, without your work, will appear. In some parts of the chapter, you will be asked to sign out of the Sample Company and then sign back in so the Sample Company is reset to its original state. In the end of chapter work, you will be asked to perform the same tasks completed on the Sample Company on your Student Company. That work, of course, will be saved.

Budget Creation

In this section, you will be establishing a Profit and Loss budget in QBO, which tracks amounts in income and expense accounts. QBO will interview you to determine budget amounts. You will be creating your budget from scratch since you have no historical amounts in QBO.

To create a Profit and Loss budget for the Sample Company, do the following:

1 Open your Internet browser.

2 Type **https://qbo.intuit.com/redir/testdrive** into your browser's address text box, and press [**Enter**] to view the Sample Company Home page.

3 Click the **Gear** icon, and select **Budgeting** shown in Figure 8.1.

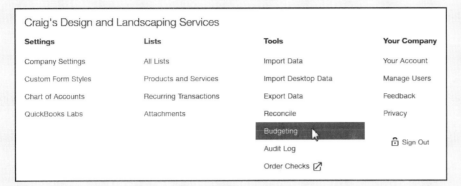

Figure 8.1

Budgeting window (accessing the budgeting process)

4 Read page 1 of the Creating a budget instructions, and click **Next**.

5 Select the option button titled **No amounts. Create budget from scratch** shown in Figure 8.2.

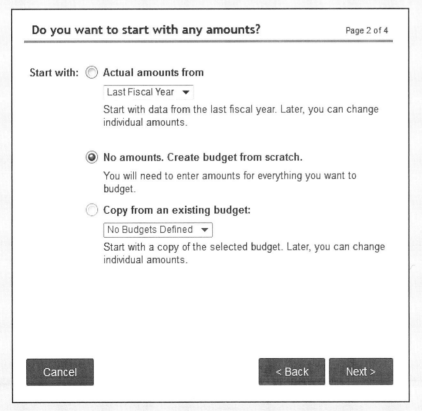

Figure 8.2

Creating a budget from scratch

6   Click **Next.**

7   Select the option button titled **Don't subdivide**, and click **Next.**

8   Leave the default fiscal year provided, and type **Budget 1** as the Budget name. (The default fiscal year will change based on the date you use for the Sample Company. Thus, the dates in QBO will not match the dates shown in the text figures for the Sample Company.)

9   Click **Finish.** Then click **Finished.** Now click the **Gear** icon and then click **Budgeting.**

10 When the budget worksheet appears, click in the **Design income** account, which will activate the Edit – Design income section at the bottom of the worksheet.

11 Type **3000** in the Jan: text box, then click the **Copy Across** button as shown in Figure 8.3.

Figure 8.3

Profit and Loss
(budget worksheet)

12 Click **Save & Next** to view Figure 8.4.

Figure 8.4

Profit and Loss (design income
budget amounts)

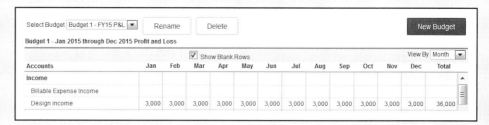

13 Scroll down the budget worksheet as needed to enter the amounts shown in Figure 8.5.

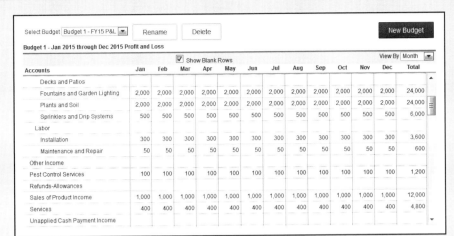

Figure 8.5

Profit and Loss (budget worksheet)

14 After entering the above amounts, click **Finished**. (This needs to be done even though you are not finished so QBO doesn't time out and make you start again.)

15 Click the **Gear** icon, and select **Budgeting** to continue the process.

16 Scroll down the budget worksheet, and add additional <u>monthly</u> amounts for cost of goods sold: **400**, advertising: **100**, automobile: **500**, equipment rental: **100**, insurance: **250**, job expenses: **1,000**, legal and professional: **950**, maintenance and repair: **900**, rent or lease: **800**, utilities: **500**, Miscellaneous: **3,000**.

17 Click **Finished**.

You have entered budgeted amounts and stored them in QBO. Now, view budget reports.

Budget Reports

QBO has two basic budget-related reports: Budget Overview and Budget vs. Actual. The overview report only lists budget data. The Budget vs. Actual lists budget data compared to actual transactions inputted into QBO.

To view budget reports in the Sample Company, do the following:

1 Continue from where you left off.

2 Click the **Reports**, type **Budget** in the Go to report text box.

3 Select **Budget Overview**, and click **Collapse** to view the collapsed Budget Overview report for the year shown in Figure 8.6.

Figure 8.6

Budget Overview
(collapsed report)

Craig's Design and Landscaping Services
BUDGET OVERVIEW

	TOTAL
Income	
Design income	36,000.00
Landscaping Services	58,200.00
Pest Control Services	1,200.00
Sales of Product Income	12,000.00
Services	4,800.00
Total Income	**$112,200.00**
Cost of Goods Sold	
Cost of Goods Sold	4,800.00
Total Cost of Goods Sold	**$4,800.00**
Gross Profit	**$107,400.00**
Expenses	
Advertising	1,200.00
Automobile	6,000.00
Equipment Rental	1,200.00
Insurance	3,000.00
Job Expenses	12,000.00
Legal & Professional Fees	11,400.00
Maintenance and Repair	10,800.00
Rent or Lease	9,600.00
Utilities	6,000.00
Total Expenses	**$61,200.00**
Net Operating Income	**$46,200.00**
Other Expenses	
Miscellaneous	36,000.00
Total Other Expenses	**$36,000.00**
Net Other Income	**$ -36,000.00**
Net Income	**$10,200.00**

4 Click **Customize** to modify the Budget Overview report.

5 Change the From: and To: dates to the current month and year (In this case, the new From: is 7/1/15 and the new To: is 7/31/15. If your current system date, today's date, is, for example, 10/8/16, you would change the From: to 10/1/16 and the To: to 10/31/16.)

6 Select **Accounts vs. Total** in the drop-down list in the Show Grid text box. See Figure 8.7 as an example.

Figure 8.7

Customizing Budget Overview

Customize Budget Overview

General	General
Rows/Columns	Budget: Budget 1 - FY15 P&L ▼
Lists	Transaction Date: Custom ▼
Numbers	From: 07/01/2015 📅 To: 07/31/2015 📅
Header/Footer	Rows/Columns
	Show Grid: Accounts vs. Total ▼

7 Click **Run Report** to view the customized Budget Overview report shown in Figure 8.8.

Craig's Design and Landscaping Services
BUDGET OVERVIEW: BUDGET 1 - FY15 P&L
July 2015

	TOTAL
Income	
Design income	3,000.00
Landscaping Services	4,850.00
Pest Control Services	100.00
Sales of Product Income	1,000.00
Services	400.00
Total Income	**$9,350.00**
Cost of Goods Sold	
Cost of Goods Sold	400.00
Total Cost of Goods Sold	**$400.00**
Gross Profit	**$8,950.00**
Expenses	
Advertising	100.00
Automobile	500.00
Equipment Rental	100.00
Insurance	250.00
Job Expenses	1,000.00
Legal & Professional Fees	950.00
Maintenance and Repair	900.00
Rent or Lease	800.00
Utilities	500.00
Total Expenses	**$5,100.00**
Net Operating Income	**$3,850.00**
Other Expenses	
Miscellaneous	3,000.00
Total Other Expenses	**$3,000.00**
Net Other Income	**$ -3,000.00**
Net Income	**$850.00**

Figure 8.8

Budget Overview
(customized report)

8 Click **Save Customizations**, type **Budget Overview** in the Name of custom report text box, check **Share this report with all company users** check box, and click **OK**.

9 Click the **Reports**, and click **Budget vs. Actuals** from the list of recommended reports.

10 Click **Collapse**.

11 Click **Customize** to modify the Budget vs. Actual report.

12 Change the From: and To: dates to the current previous month and year. (In this case, the new From: is 6/1/15 and the new To: is 6/30/15. If your current system date, today's date, is, for example, 10/8/16, you would change the From: to 9/1/16 and the To: to 9/30/16.)

13 Select **Accounts vs. Total** in the drop-down list in the Show Grid text box. See Figure 8.9 as an example.

Figure 8.9

Customizing Budget vs. Actuals

Customize Budget vs. Actuals

General

Budget: Budget 1 - FY15 P&L ▾

Transaction Date: Custom ▾

From: 06/01/2015   To: 06/30/2015

Accounting Method: ◯ Cash Basis
               ◉ Accrual

☐ Only accounts with budgeted amounts

Rows/Columns

Show Grid: Accounts vs. Total ▾

14 Click **Run Report** to view the customized Budget vs. Actuals report shown in Figure 8.10. Note: your budget amounts should match this figure but your actual amounts will be different since the actual data changes based on when you are using the Sample company.

Figure 8.10

Budget vs. Actual Report

Craig's Design and Landscaping Services
BUDGET VS. ACTUALS: BUDGET 1 - FY15 P&L
June 2015

	ACTUAL	BUDGET	OVER BUDGET	% OF BUDGET
Income				
Design income	2,250.00	3,000.00	-750.00	75.00 %
Discounts given	-89.50		-89.50	
Landscaping Services	4,799.72	4,850.00	-50.28	98.96 %
Pest Control Services	-30.00	100.00	-130.00	-30.00 %
Sales of Product Income	912.75	1,000.00	-87.25	91.28 %
Services	503.55	400.00	103.55	125.89 %
Total Income	**$8,346.52**	**$9,350.00**	**$ -1,003.48**	**89.27 %**
Cost of Goods Sold				
Cost of Goods Sold	405.00	400.00	5.00	101.25 %
Total Cost of Goods Sold	**$405.00**	**$400.00**	**$5.00**	**101.25 %**
Gross Profit	**$7,941.52**	**$8,950.00**	**$ -1,008.48**	**88.73 %**
Expenses				
Advertising	74.86	100.00	-25.14	74.86 %
Automobile	272.83	500.00	-227.17	54.57 %
Equipment Rental	112.00	100.00	12.00	112.00 %
Insurance	241.23	250.00	-8.77	96.49 %
Job Expenses	560.23	1,000.00	-439.77	56.02 %
Legal & Professional Fees	565.00	950.00	-385.00	59.47 %
Maintenance and Repair	940.00	900.00	40.00	104.44 %
Meals and Entertainment	9.52		9.52	
Office Expenses	18.08		18.08	
Rent or Lease	900.00	800.00	100.00	112.50 %
Utilities	188.45	500.00	-311.55	37.69 %
Total Expenses	**$3,882.20**	**$5,100.00**	**$ -1,217.80**	**76.12 %**
Net Operating Income	**$4,059.32**	**$3,850.00**	**$209.32**	**105.44 %**
Other Expenses				
Miscellaneous	2,666.00	3,000.00	-334.00	88.87 %
Total Other Expenses	**$2,666.00**	**$3,000.00**	**$ -334.00**	**88.87 %**
Net Other Income	**$ -2,666.00**	**$ -3,000.00**	**$334.00**	**88.87 %**
Net Income	**$1,393.32**	**$850.00**	**$543.32**	**163.92 %**

15   Click **Save Customizations**, type **Budget vs. Actuals** in the Name of custom report text box, check **Share this report with all company users** check box, and click **OK**.

16   Sign out of the Sample Company.

Bank Reconciliation

Good internal control requires frequent reconciliations between bank records and a company's records of cash receipts and payments completed by someone other than the accountant or bookkeeper who is responsible for maintaining accounting records. The process involves comparing items that appear in the checking account with those items appearing on the bank statement. Deposits that appear in the checking account but do not appear on the bank statement are referred to as deposits in transit. Checks that appear in the checking account but do not appear on the bank statement are referred to as outstanding checks. They usually appear as checks on the next bank statement.

In QBO, if you discover a deposit recorded by the bank but not recorded in the checking account (determined to be an error in the checking account), you should correct the checking account by recording the deposit. Likewise, if you discover a check recorded by the bank but not recorded in the checking account (determined to be an error in the checking account), you should correct the checking account by recording the check. In the example below, neither was identified.

To create reconciliation for the Sample Company, do the following:

1   Open your Internet browser.

2   Type **https://qbo.intuit.com/redir/testdrive** into your browser's address text box, and press [**Enter**] to view the Sample Company Home page.

3   Click the **Gear** icon, and select **Reconcile** as shown in Figure 8.11.

Figure 8.11

Reconciliation process (access)

4   Make sure the **Checking** account is selected in the Reconcile window shown in Figure 8.12.

Figure 8.12

Reconcile window

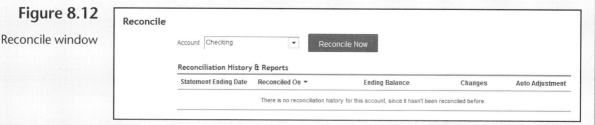

5   Click **Reconcile Now**.

6   Type **6/30/15** as the Statement Ending Date, and type **1822.86** as the Ending Balance. Your date will differ depending on your current system date. Usually, you will need to input the last day of the month from the month prior to your current system date.

7   Click **OK** to view the Reconcile – Checking form shown in Figure 8.13.

Figure 8.13

Reconcile – Checking form

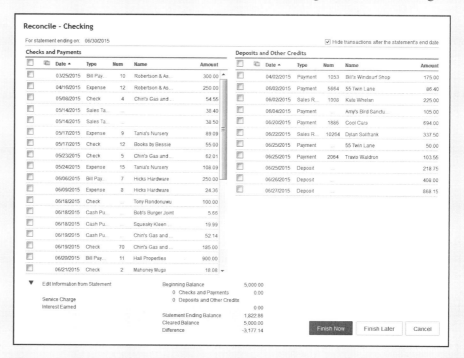

8   After a review of the company's most recent bank statement and a comparison with the company's checking account, you discover some checks and payments recorded in the checking account that did not appear on the bank statement. Place a check next to all checks and payments except for check **13** to Hicks Hardware for 215.66, check **75** to Hicks Hardware for 228.75, and check **76** to Pam Seitz for 75.00, none of which had cleared the bank.

9   After a review of the company's most recent bank statement and a comparison with the company's checking account, you discover some deposits and other credits recorded in the checking account that did not appear on the bank statement. Place a check next to all deposits and other credits <u>except</u> for payment **1886** from Cool Cars for 694.00

and payment **2064** from Travis Waldron for 103.55, neither of which had cleared the bank.

10 Your account is reconciled as shown by the 0.00 difference between the Statement Ending Balance and the Cleared Balance shown in Figure 8.14. Be sure all the items referenced in the above steps (checks and payments as well as deposits and other credits) are properly checked or unchecked.

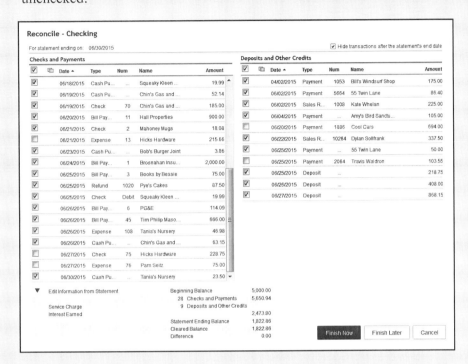

Figure 8.14

Reconcile–Checking form (reconciled account)

11 Once you have reconciled the checking account, click **Finish Now**.

12 A summary of all reconciliation reports completed should appear shown in Figure 8.15.

Figure 8.15

Reconcile (reconciliation summary)

13 Click on the reconciliation ending balance **1,822.86** to view the reconciliation report. The upper summary portion of that report is shown in Figure 8.16.

Figure 8.16

Summary Reconciliation Report

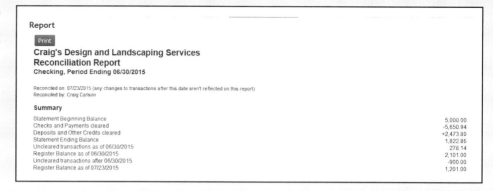

14   Click **Print**, click **OK**, and click **Close** to print the report and close its window.

15   Sign out of the Sample Company.

End Note

In this chapter, you created a Profit and Loss budget for 12 months, prepared a Budget Overview report and Budget vs. Actual report, and reconciled your checking account. In the next chapter, you will work with adjusting journal entries.

Chapter 8 Questions

1   What are the steps to create a Profit and Loss budget?

2   What value do budgets provide a business?

3   Why should a business reconcile a checking account?

4   Who should prepare a bank reconciliation?

5   What options are available when creating a budget other than creating one from scratch?

6   What button is used to replicate amounts across several months in the budget worksheet?

7   How do you know if you have correctly reconciled an account?

8   What are the steps to change a Budget Overview report from covering a year to covering just one month?

9   What should you do if you discover a deposit was recorded by the bank but not recorded in the checking account (determined to be an error in the checking account)?

10   What are the steps to print a bank reconciliation report?

Chapter 8 Matching

a.   Budget Overview report   _____ Condenses a report

b.   Budget vs. Actual report   _____ Do not appear on the bank statement

c.   Deposits in transit   _____ Used to change report dates

d.   Outstanding checks   _____ Includes only budget amounts

e.   Collapse   _____ Usually appear as checks on the next bank statement

f.   Customize   _____ Includes both budget and actual amounts

Chapter 8 Cases

The following cases require you to open the company you updated in Chapter 7. Each case below continues throughout the text in a sequential manner. For example, if you are assigned Case 1, you will use the file you modified in this chapter in all following chapters. Each case below is similar in concepts assessed but differs in amounts and transactions.

To reopen your company, do the following:

1   Open your Internet browser.

2   Type **https://qbo.intuit.com/qbo28/login?webredir** into your browser's address text box.

3   Type your User ID and Password into the text boxes as you have done before.

Case 1

Based on what you learned in the text, using the Sample Company, you are to add the following activities to your company:

1 Add an invoice on 1/30/18 to customer: Blondie's Boards, terms: Net 30, for 4 Fred Rubbles, 7 Water Hogs, and 8 Rook 15 surf boards.

2 Add an invoice on 1/31/18 to a new customer: Surf Rider Foundation, terms: net 30, for 100 hours of consulting.

3 Add the following FY 2018 (Jan 2018 – Dec 2018) monthly budgeted amounts as you did earlier in the chapter: sales: 40,000, services: 3,000, cost of goods sold: 23,500, interest expense: 600, payroll: 12,000, rent or lease: 2500, travel: 500, utilities: 200. Amounts provided should be input for each month of 2018. Use Budget 1 as the budget name.

4 Create and customize, save customization as Budget Overview Budget 1, print, and export to Excel a Budget Overview report for the month of January 2018. Your report should look like Figure 8.17.

Figure 8.17

Budget Overview (January 2018)

Case 1
BUDGET OVERVIEW: BUDGET 1 - FY18 P&L
January 2018

	TOTAL
Income	
Sales	40,000.00
Services	3,000.00
Total Income	$43,000.00
Cost of Goods Sold	
Cost of Goods Sold	23,500.00
Total Cost of Goods Sold	$23,500.00
Gross Profit	$19,500.00
Expenses	
Interest Expense	600.00
Payroll	12,000.00
Rent or Lease	2,500.00
Travel	500.00
Utilities	200.00
Total Expenses	$15,800.00
Net Operating Income	$3,700.00
Net Income	$3,700.00

5 Create and customize, save customization as Budget vs. Actual Budget 1, print, and export to Excel a Budget vs. Actuals report for the month of January 2018. Your report should look like Figure 8.18.

Figure 8.18

Budget vs. Actuals (January 2018)

Case 1
BUDGET VS. ACTUALS: BUDGET 1 - FY18 P&L
January 2018

	TOTAL			
	ACTUAL	BUDGET	OVER BUDGET	% OF BUDGET
Income				
Sales	17,180.00	40,000.00	-22,820.00	42.95 %
Services	2,670.00	3,000.00	-330.00	89.00 %
Total Income	$19,850.00	$43,000.00	$ -23,150.00	46.16 %
Cost of Goods Sold				
Cost of Goods Sold	10,400.00	23,500.00	-13,100.00	44.26 %
Total Cost of Goods Sold	$10,400.00	$23,500.00	$ -13,100.00	44.26 %
Gross Profit	$9,450.00	$19,500.00	$ -10,050.00	48.46 %
Expenses				
Interest Expense	600.00	600.00	0.00	100.00 %
Payroll	11,785.71	12,000.00	-214.29	98.21 %
Rent or Lease	2,500.00	2,500.00	0.00	100.00 %
Travel	1,800.00	500.00	1,300.00	360.00 %
Utilities	145.00	200.00	-55.00	72.50 %
Total Expenses	$16,830.71	$15,800.00	$1,030.71	106.52 %
Net Operating Income	$ -7,380.71	$3,700.00	$ -11,080.71	-199.48 %
Net Income	$ -7,380.71	$3,700.00	$ -11,080.71	-199.48 %

6 Open and print the custom report you created in the last chapter called Transaction Detail by Account.

7 Export your Transactions Detail by Account report to Excel and save it with the file name: Student Name (replace with your name) Ch 08 Case 01 Transaction Detail by Account.xlsx.

8 Reconcile your company's checking account. No services charges were incurred or interest earned. The ending bank statement balance on 1/31/18 was $29,202.37.

9 After a review of the company's most recent bank statement and a comparison with the company's checking account, you discover some checks and payments recorded in the checking account that did not appear on the bank statement. Place a check next to all checks and payments <u>except</u> for check **1009** to Ben Franklin for 3,113.22 and check **1010** to Betsy Ross for 1,149.87, neither of which had cleared the bank.

10 After a review of the company's most recent bank statement and a comparison with the company's checking account, you discover some deposits and other credits recorded in the checking account that did not appear on the bank statement. Place a check next to all deposits and other credits <u>except</u> for a deposit on 1/8/18 from Blondie's Boards for 1,300.00, which had not cleared the bank.

11 Print the resulting Reconciliation Report.

12 Sign out of your company.

Case 2

Based on what you learned in the text and using the Sample Company, you are to add the following activities to your company:

1 Add an invoice on 1/30/19 to customer: Hagen's Toys, terms: Net 30, for 100 hours of custom painting.

2 Add an invoice on 1/31/19 to a new customer: Zack's RC, terms: net 30, for 2 Seawind Carbon Sailboats and 2 Mystique RES.

3 Add the following FY 2019 (Jan 2019 – Dec 2019) <u>monthly</u> budgeted amounts like you did in the chapter: sales: 10,000, services: 4,000, cost of goods sold: 5,000, advertising: 500, insurance: 425, interest expense: 300, meals and entertainment: 250, and payroll: 9,000. Amounts provided should be input for each month of 2019. Use Budget 1 as the budget name.

4 Create and customize, save customization as Budget Overview Budget 1, print, and export to Excel a Budget Overview report for the month of January 2019. Your report should look like Figure 8.19.

Figure 8.19

Budget Overview (January 2019)

Case 2 BUDGET OVERVIEW: BUDGET 1 - FY19 P&L January 2019	
	TOTAL
Income	
Sales	10,000.00
Services	4,000.00
Total Income	$14,000.00
Cost of Goods Sold	
Cost of Goods Sold	5,000.00
Total Cost of Goods Sold	$5,000.00
Gross Profit	$9,000.00
Expenses	
Advertising	500.00
Insurance	425.00
Interest Expense	300.00
Meals and Entertainment	250.00
Payroll	9,000.00
Total Expenses	$10,475.00
Net Operating Income	$ -1,475.00
Net Income	$ -1,475.00

5 Create and customize, save customization as Budget vs. Actuals Budget 1, print, and export to Excel a Budget vs. Actuals report for the month of January 2019. Your report should look like Figure 8.20.

Case 2
BUDGET VS. ACTUALS: BUDGET 1 - FY19 P&L
January 2019

	TOTAL			
	ACTUAL	BUDGET	OVER BUDGET	% OF BUDGET
Income				
Sales	9,000.00	10,000.00	-1,000.00	90.00 %
Services	4,725.00	4,000.00	725.00	118.13 %
Total Income	**$13,725.00**	**$14,000.00**	**$ -275.00**	**98.04 %**
Cost of Goods Sold				
Cost of Goods Sold	4,910.00	5,000.00	-90.00	98.20 %
Total Cost of Goods Sold	**$4,910.00**	**$5,000.00**	**$ -90.00**	**98.20 %**
Gross Profit	**$8,815.00**	**$9,000.00**	**$ -185.00**	**97.94 %**
Expenses				
Advertising	500.00	500.00	0.00	100.00 %
Insurance	400.00	425.00	-25.00	94.12 %
Interest Expense	300.00	300.00	0.00	100.00 %
Meals and Entertainment	240.00	250.00	-10.00	96.00 %
Payroll	9,224.26	9,000.00	224.26	102.49 %
Total Expenses	**$10,664.26**	**$10,475.00**	**$189.26**	**101.81 %**
Net Operating Income	**$ -1,849.26**	**$ -1,475.00**	**$ -374.26**	**125.37 %**
Net Income	**$ -1,849.26**	**$ -1,475.00**	**$ -374.26**	**125.37 %**

Figure 8.20

Budget vs. Actuals (January 2019)

6   Open and print the custom report you created in the last chapter called Transaction Detail by Account.

7   Export your Transactions Detail by Account report to Excel and save it with the file name: Student Name (replace with your name) Ch 08 Case 02 Transaction Detail by Account.xlsx.

8   Reconcile your company's checking account. No services charges were incurred or interest earned. The ending bank statement balance on 1/31/19 was $30,693.47.

9   After a review of the company's most recent bank statement and a comparison with the company's checking account, you discover some checks and payments recorded in the checking account that did not appear on the bank statement. Place a check next to all checks and payments <u>except</u> for check **1009** to Frank Benjamin for 2,359.50 and check **1010** to Sara Juarez for 973.29, neither of which had cleared the bank.

10   After a review of the company's most recent bank statement and a comparison with the company's checking account, you discover a deposit and other credit recorded in the checking account that did not appear on the bank statement. Place a check next to all deposits and other credits <u>except</u> for a deposit on 1/7/19 from Benson's RC for 4,500.00, which had not cleared the bank.

11   Print the resulting Reconciliation Report.

12   Sign out of your company.

9

Adjusting Entries

Student Learning Outcomes

Upon completion of this chapter, the student will be able to do the following:

- Prepare an unadjusted trial balance
- Make adjusting entries for the following:
  - Prepaid expenses
  - Accrued expenses
  - Unearned revenue
  - Accrued revenue
  - Depreciation

Overview

Intuit has provided a Sample Company online to let new users test drive its QBO product. In this chapter, you will open this Sample Company and practice adjusting entry activities in QBO. Prior to the creation of periodic financial statements, generally accepted accounting principles (GAAP) require that accounting records be adjusted to reflect accrual accounting. This process insures revenues are recorded in the period in which they are earned and that expenses are recorded in the period in which they were consumed. In the process, expenses will be matched in the same period to the revenues generated from incurring those expenses.

There are five types of adjusting entries. Expenses paid, prior to being consumed, should be deferred (such as supplies, rent, insurance, etc.) and recorded as assets (such as supplies asset, prepaid rent, and prepaid insurance, etc.) until they are consumed. To defer is to postpone. Expenses incurred prior to being paid (payroll, rent, utilities, etc.) must be recorded and accrued as a liability. To accrue is to increase. Revenue collected prior to being earned must be deferred (such as sales, services, etc.) and recorded as liabilities (such as unearned revenue) until they are earned. Revenues earned prior to being collected (sales and services, etc.) must be recorded and accrued as a receivable. Lastly, fixed assets (buildings, furniture, equipment, vehicles etc.) must be depreciated over their useful life to match costs with revenues.

Remember, if you stop in the middle of this work, none of your work will be saved. So, when you return, the same sample company, without your work, will appear. In some parts of the chapter, you will be asked to sign out of the Sample Company and sign back in so the Sample Company is reset to its original state. In the end of chapter work, you will be asked to perform the same tasks completed on the Sample Company on your Student Company. That work, of course, will be saved.

Trial Balance

In this section, you will create a trial balance (before adjusting entries), which must be analyzed in light of end of the period business events to determine the required adjusting entries.

To create a trial balance for the Sample Company, do the following:

1 Open your Internet browser.

2 Type **https://qbo.intuit.com/redir/testdrive** into your browser's address text box and the press [**Enter**] to view the Sample Company Home page.

3 Click **Reports** from the navigation bar.

4 Type **Trial Balance** in the Go to report search box and the press [**Enter**].

5 Change the To: date to the last day of the current month (in this case **7/31/15**, your date will be different) then click **Run Report** to view the trial balance shown in Figure 9.1.

Craig's Design and Landscaping Services
TRIAL BALANCE
As of July 31, 2015

	DEBIT	CREDIT
Checking	1,201.00	
Savings	800.00	
Accounts Receivable (A/R)	5,281.52	
Inventory Asset	596.25	
Undeposited Funds	2,062.52	
Truck:Original Cost	13,495.00	
Accounts Payable (A/P)		1,602.67
Mastercard		157.72
Arizona Dept. of Revenue Payable		0.00
Board of Equalization Payable		370.94
Loan Payable		4,000.00
Notes Payable		25,000.00
Opening Balance Equity	9,337.50	
Design income		2,250.00
Discounts given	89.50	
Landscaping Services		1,477.50
Landscaping Services:Job Materials:Fountains and Garden Lighting		2,246.50
Landscaping Services:Job Materials:Plants and Soil		2,351.97
Landscaping Services:Job Materials:Sprinklers and Drip Systems		138.00
Landscaping Services:Labor:Installation		250.00
Landscaping Services:Labor:Maintenance and Repair		50.00
Pest Control Services		110.00
Sales of Product Income		912.75
Services		503.55
Cost of Goods Sold	405.00	

Figure 9.1

Trial Balance report (partial view)

Adjusting Journal Entries: Prepaid Expenses

Further investigation of this trial balance and period end business activities indicates that $500 of supplies were recorded as a miscellaneous expense but should have been deferred as a supplies asset until consumed in some future period. Thus, an adjusting entry is necessary.

To record an adjusting entry for supplies in the Sample Company, do the following:

1 Continue from where you left off. If you closed the Sample Company, follow the steps to re-open it found at the beginning of this chapter.

2 Click the **Create** + icon, and click **Journal Entry**.

3 Type the last day of the current month into the **Journal date** text box (in this case 7/31/15).

4 Type **Supplies Asset** on line 1 of the Account column, and click + **Add Supplies Asset** shown in Figure 9.2. (This is another way to add a new account in QBO.)

Figure 9.2

Journal entry (adding a new account)

5 Select **Other Current Assets** from the drop-down list in the **Category Type** text box.

6 Select **Prepaid Expenses** from the drop-down list in the **Detail Type** text box.

7 Click **Save and Close**.

8 Type **500** into the Debit column of line 1.

9 Select **Miscellaneous** from the drop-down list in line 2 of the Accounts column.

10 Accept **500** into the Credit column of line 2 to view the journal entry shown in Figure 9.3.

Figure 9.3

Journal Entry #1 (to defer supplies)

11 Click **Save and Close**.

The same process could be used to defer a cost that had been recorded as an expense but should be deferred as an asset at period end. Examples might include insurance to be deferred as either prepaid insurance or prepaid expenses or as rent be deferred as either prepaid rent or prepaid expenses.

Another example of this occurs when an expense is deferred in a prior period but is consumed in the current period. We will use the Supplies Asset created as an example assuming $100 of supplies were consumed in the month leaving $400 of supplies as an asset.

To record an adjusting journal entry to record the consumption of supplies, do the following:

1 Continue from where you left off. If you closed the Sample Company, follow the steps to re-open it found at the beginning of this chapter.

2 Click the **Create +** icon and then click **Journal Entry**.

3 Type the last day of the current month into the **Journal date** text box (in this case 7/31/15).

4 Select **Supplies** from the drop-down list in line 1 of the Account column. (This is an expense account already in the Company's chart of accounts.)

5 Type **100** into the Debit column of line 1.

6 Select **Supplies Asset** from the drop-down list in line 2 of the Accounts column.

7 Accept **100** into the Credit column of line 2 to view the journal entry shown in Figure 9.4.

Figure 9.4

Journal entry (recording the consumption of supplies)

Journal Entry #2

Journal date					Journal no.
07/31/2015					2

	#	ACCOUNT	DEBITS	CREDITS	DESCRIPTION
⠿	1	Supplies	100.00		
⠿	2	Supplies Asset		100.00	

8 **Click Save and Close**.

9 Closing the journal entry should reveal the trial balance created before but updated to reflect the supplies asset account shown in Figure 9.5.

Figure 9.5

Trial Balance after supplies adjustments (partial view)

Craig's Design and Landscaping Services
TRIAL BALANCE
As of July 31, 2015

	DEBIT	CREDIT
Checking	1,201.00	
Savings	800.00	
Accounts Receivable (A/R)	5,281.52	
Inventory Asset	596.25	
Supplies Asset	400.00	
Undeposited Funds	2,062.52	
Truck:Original Cost	13,495.00	

10 Click the Supplies Asset **400.00** amount to reveal a Transaction Report for the Supplies Asset account shown in Figure 9.6.

11 Click **Back to Summary Report** to return to the Trial Balance report.

Figure 9.6

Transaction Report (for supplies asset)

Craig's Design and Landscaping Services
TRANSACTION REPORT
July 2015

DATE	TRANSACTION TYPE	NUM	NAME	MEMO/DESCRIPTION	ACCOUNT	SPLIT	AMOUNT	BALANCE
Supplies Asset								
07/31/2015	Journal Entry	1			Supplies Asset	-Split-	500.00	500.00
07/31/2015	Journal Entry	2			Supplies Asset	-Split-	-100.00	400.00
Total for Supplies Asset							$400.00	
TOTAL							$400.00	

The first entry deferred $500 from miscellaneous expense; the second entry recorded the consumption of supplies reducing the asset account.

Adjusting Journal Entries: Accrued Expenses

Further investigation of this trial balance and period end business activities indicates that a bill for $300 was received and recorded in the next month for advertising consumed in the current month. Thus, an adjusting journal entry needs to be made to accrue this expense. For our purposes, we will create a new accrued liabilities account to keep track of these accruals and keep them separate from accounts payable.

To record an adjusting journal entry to record the accrual of advertising expense, do the following:

1   Continue from where you left off. If you closed the Sample Company, follow the steps to re-open it found at the beginning of this chapter.

2   Click the **Create + icon**, and click **Journal Entry**.

3   Type the last day of the current month into the Journal date text box (in this case 7/31/15).

4   Select **Advertising** from the drop-down list in line 1 of the Account column.

5   Type **300** into the Debits column of line 1.

6   Type **Accrued Liabilities** on line 2 of the Account column and then click **+ Add Accrued Liabilities**

7   Select **Other Current Liabilities** from the drop-down list in the **Category Type** text box.

8   Select **Other Current Liabilities** from the drop-down list in the **Detail Type** text box.

9   Click **Save and Close**.

10 Accept **300** into the Credits column of line 2 to view the journal entry shown in Figure 9.7.

Journal date			Journal no.	
07/31/2015			3	

#	ACCOUNT	DEBITS	CREDITS	DESCRIPTION
1	Advertising	300.00		
2	Accrued Liabilities		300.00	

Figure 9.7

Journal entry (accruing advertising expense)

11 **Click Save and Close**.

12 Closing the journal entry should reveal the trial balance created before but now updated to reflect the accrual of advertising expense to the accrued liabilities account.

13 Click the Accrued Liabilities **300.00** amount to reveal a Transaction Report.

14 Click **Back to Summary Report** to return to the Trial Balance report.

Adjusting Journal Entries: Unearned Revenue

Further investigation of this trial balance and period end business activities indicates that design income recorded on sales receipt #1003 for $337.50 to Dylan Sollfrank were never performed even though cash had been received. Thus, the revenue had not been earned. Work is expected to occur next month, thus this amount of revenue must be deferred and set up as an unearned revenue liability.

To record an adjusting journal entry to reflect earned revenue, do the following:

1 Continue from where you left off. If you closed the Sample Company, follow the steps to re-open it found at the beginning of this chapter.

2 Click the **Create +** icon and then click **Journal Entry**.

3 Type the last day of the current month into the Journal date text box (in this case 7/31/15).

4 Select **Design Income** from the drop-down list in line 1 of the Account column.

5 Type **337.50** into the Debits column of line 1.

6 Select **Dylan Sollfrank** from the drop-down list of customers in the Name column of line 1.

7 Type **Unearned Revenue** on line 2 of the Account column and then click **+ Add Unearned Revenue**

8 Select **Other Current Liabilities** from the drop-down list in the **Category Type** text box.

9 Select **Other Current Liabilities** from the drop-down list in the **Detail Type** text box.

10 Click **Save and Close**.

11 Accept **337.50** into the Credits column of line 2 to view the journal entry shown in Figure 9.8.

12 Click **Save and Close**.

Figure 9.8

Journal entry (recording unearned revenue)

Journal date					Journal no.	
07/31/2015					4	

#	ACCOUNT	DEBITS	CREDITS	DESCRIPTION	NAME
1	Design income	337.50			Dylan Sollfrank
2	Unearned Revenue		337.50		

13 Closing the journal entry should reveal the trial balance created before but updated to reflect the deferral of revenue to the unearned revenue liability account.

14 Click the Unearned Revenue **337.50** amount to reveal a Transaction Report.

15 Click **Back to Summary Report** to return to the Trial Balance report.

Adjusting Journal Entries: Accruing Revenue

Further investigation of this trial balance and period end business activities indicates that some landscaping services of $500 were performed on the last day of the month for Diego Rodriguez but not invoiced to the customer or recorded into the accounting records until a few days into the next month. Thus, you will need to record an adjusting journal entry to accrue revenue and an accrued receivable.

To record an adjusting journal entry to reflect earned revenue, do the following:

1 Continue from where you left off. If you closed the Sample Company, follow the steps to re-open it found at the beginning of this chapter.

2 Click the **Create + icon** and then click **Journal Entry**.

3 Type the last day of the current month into the **Journal date** text box (in this case 7/31/15).

4 Type **Accrued Receivable** on line 1 of the Account column and then click **+ Add Accrued Receivable**

5 Select **Other Current Assets** from the drop-down list in the **Category Type** text box.

6 Select **Other Current Assets** from the drop-down list in the **Detail Type** text box.

7 Click **Save and Close**.

8 Type **500** into the Debits column of line 1.

9 Select **Diego Rodriguez** from the drop-down list of customers in the Name column of line 1

10 Select **Landscaping Services** from the drop-down list in line 2 of the Account column.

11 Accept **500** in the Credits column of line 2.

12 Select **Diego Rodriguez** from the drop-down list of customers in the Name column of line 2 to view the journal entry shown in Figure 9.9.

Journal date					Journal no.		
07/31/2015					5		

	#	ACCOUNT	DEBITS	CREDITS	DESCRIPTION	NAME
⠿	1	Accrued Receivable	500.00			Diego Rodriguez
⠿	2	Landscaping Services		500.00		Diego Rodriguez

Figure 9.9

Journal entry (recording accrued revenue)

13 Click **Save and Close**.

14 Closing the journal entry should reveal the trial balance created before but updated to reflect the accrual of revenue to the accrued receivable account.

15 Click the Accrued Receivable **500.00** amount to reveal a Transaction Report.

16 Click **Back to Summary Report** to return to the Trial Balance report.

Adjusting Journal Entries: Depreciation

Further investigation of this trial balance and period end business activities indicates the company's only fixed asset, a truck, needed to be depreciated for the month. Monthly depreciation is $1,000. Normally, the adjusting entry would debit depreciation expense and credit accumulated depreciation. However, the accounts set up in the sample company are both named depreciation. Thus, you decide to change the account names first and then record the depreciation adjusting journal entry.

To edit account names and then record an adjusting journal entry to record depreciation, do the following:

1 Continue from where you left off. If you closed the Sample Company, follow the steps to re-open it found at the beginning of this chapter.

2 Click the **Gear** icon and then click **Chart of Accounts**.

3 Click **Edit** from the drop-down arrow next to the words View register on the Depreciation line listed under the Truck account.

4 Type **Accumulated** in front of Depreciation in the **Name** text box and then click **Save and Close**.

5 Scroll down to the bottom of the chart of accounts and select **Edit** from the drop-down arrow next to the words Run report on the Depreciation line listed above Miscellaneous.

6 Type **Expense** after Depreciation in the **Name** text box and then click **Save and Close**.

7 Click the **Create +** icon and then click **Journal Entry**.

8 Type the last day of the current month into the Journal date text box (in this case 7/31/15).

9 Select **Depreciation Expense** from the drop-down list in line 1 of the Account column.

10 Type **1000** into the Debits column of line 1.

11 Select **Truck:Accumulated Depreciation** from the drop-down list in line 2 of the Accounts column.

12 Accept **1,000.00** as the Credits column amount.

13 Click **Save and close**.

14   Click **Reports** from the navigation bar and then type **Trial Balance** in the **Go to report** text box and then press [Enter] to view the trial balance.

15   Change the To: to the end of the current month like you've done before to reveal a trial balance now updated to reflect the depreciation expense and accumulated depreciation just recorded.

16   Click the Truck: Accumulated Depreciation **1,000.00** amount to reveal a Transaction Report.

17   Click **Back to Summary Report** to return to the Trial Balance report.

End Note

In this chapter, you recorded adjusting entries to create accrual accounting based records. In the next chapter, you will create financial statements and useful reports.

Chapter 9 Questions

1 What is an unadjusted trial balance?

2 What is an adjusted trial balance?

3 Why accrue an expense?

4 Why defer an expense?

5 Why accrue revenues?

6 Why defer revenues?

7 What QBO task is used to record accruals and deferrals?

8 Why depreciate a fixed asset?

9 Describe the new method you learned in this chapter to add a new account from within a journal entry.

10 Describe the new method you learned in this chapter to add a new customer or vendor from within a journal entry.

Chapter 9 Matching

a. Prepaid Expenses   _____ Debit this account when recording depreciation

b. Accrued Expenses   _____ Credit this account when accruing an expense

c. Unearned Revenue   _____ Debit this account when accruing revenue

d. Accrued Revenue   _____ Supplies consumed

e. Depreciation Expense   _____ Credit this account when recording depreciation

f. Supplies Asset   _____ Expenses not yet consumed

g. Supplies Expense   _____ Revenue not yet earned

h. Accrued Receivables   _____ To increase

i. Accrued Liabilities   _____ Supplies not yet consumed

j. Accumulate Depreciation _____ To postpone

Chapter 9 Cases

The following cases require you to open the company you updated in Chapter 8. Each case below continues throughout the text in a sequential manner. For example, if you are assigned Case 1, you will use the file you modified in this chapter in all following chapters. Each case below is similar in concepts assessed but differs in amounts and transactions.

To reopen your company, do the following:

1 Open your Internet browser.

2 Type **https://qbo.intuit.com/qbo28/login?webredir** into your browser's address text box.

3 Type your User ID and Password into the text boxes as you've done before.

Case 1

Based on what you learned in the text and using the Sample Company, you are to add the following activities to your company:

1 Open and review your previously customized report named Trial Balance 1/31/18.

2 Record the appropriate adjusting journal entries on 1/31/18 based on the following:

    a. An inventory of supplies reveals that only $75 of supplies remain as of 1/31/18.

    b. $800 of prepaid expenses expired (representing prepaid rent) in the month of January.

    c. A bill for $150 was received and recorded in the next month for repairs and maintenance consumed in the current month. Create a new liability account as you did earlier in the chapter.

    d. Consulting services recorded on sales receipt #1004 for $2,500.00 to Surf Rider Foundation were never performed even though cash had been received. Thus, the revenue had not been earned. Create a new liability account as you did earlier in the chapter.

    e. Consulting services of $8,500 were performed on the last day of the month for a new customer: Blazing Boards but not invoiced to the customer or recorded into the accounting records until a few days into the next month. Create a new asset account as you did earlier in the chapter.

    f. Depreciation Expense of $575 ($75 and $500 for Equipment and Furniture & Fixtures respectively) needed to be recorded for the month. Before recording this journal entry, edit the "Depreciation" expense account so that the new name is "Depreciation Expense". Also, change the account title for Furniture & Fixtures accumulated depreciation from "Depreciation" to "Accumulated Depreciation" as you did earlier in the chapter.

3 Open, print, and export to Excel your previously customized report named Trial Balance 1/31/18 which should now reflect your adjusting journal entries.

4 Open, print, and export to Excel your previously customized report named Transaction Detail by Account which should now reflect your adjusting journal entries.

Case 2

Based on what you learned in the text and using the Sample Company, you are to add the following activities to your company:

1 Open and review your previously customized report named Trial Balance 1/31/19.

2 Record the appropriate adjusting journal entries on 1/31/19 based on the following:

a. An inventory of supplies reveals that only $200 of supplies remain as of 1/31/19.

b. $1,800 of prepaid expenses expired (representing prepaid insurance) in the month of January.

c. A bill for $750 was received and recorded in the next month for legal fees performed in the current month. Create a new liability account as you did earlier in the chapter.

d. Custom painting services recorded on invoice #1003 for $4,500.00 to Hagen's toys were never performed even though invoiced. Thus, the revenue had not been earned. Create a new liability account as you did earlier in the chapter.

e. Repair services of $6,298 were performed on the last day of the month for a new customer: Kelly's Awesome Copters but not invoiced to the customer or recorded into the accounting records until a few days into the next month. Create a new asset account as you did earlier in the chapter.

f. Depreciation Expense of $1,000 ($375 and $625 for Furniture and Machinery & Equipment respectively) needed to be recorded for the month. Before recording this journal entry edit the "Depreciation" expense account so the new name is "Depreciation Expense". Also, change the account title for Machinery & Equipment accumulated depreciation from "Depreciation" to "Accumulated Depreciation" like you did in the chapter.

3 Open, print, and export to Excel your previously customized report named Trial Balance 1/31/19, which should reflect your adjusting journal entries.

4 Open, print, and export to Excel your previously customized report named Transaction Detail by Account, which should reflect your adjusting journal entries

Financial Statements and Reports

10

Upon completion of this chapter, the student will be able to do the following:

- Create an income statement
- Create a balance sheet
- Create a statement of cash flows
- Create an accounts receivable aging summary
- Create an accounts payable aging summary
- Create an inventory valuation summary
- Customize and save reports

Overview

Intuit has provided a Sample Company online to let new users test drive its QBO product. In this chapter, you will open this Sample Company and practice creating reports in QBO. Prior to the creation of periodic financial statements, generally accepted accounting principles (GAAP) require that accounting records be adjusted to reflect accrual accounting. You completed that process in the previous chapter.

Four standard reports exist in financial accounting: the income statement, the statement of stockholders' equity, the balance sheet, and the statement of cash flows. QBO does not have a report for stockholders' equity. It does have the others along with a host of other reports so you can understand the underlying business events that have occurred during a particular accounting period. You will be exploring the A/R Aging Summary, A/P Aging Summary, and Inventory Valuation Summary reports. You will also be customizing them by adding columns, removing cents,

Remember, if you stop in the middle of this work, none of your work will be saved. So, when you return, the same sample company, without your work, will appear. In some parts of the chapter, you will be asked to sign out of the Sample Company and sign back in so the Sample Company is reset to its original state. In the end of chapter work, you will be asked to perform the same tasks completed on the Sample Company on your Student Company. That work, of course, will be saved.

Income Statement

In this section, you will create an income statement. Intuit decided years ago to call this report Profit and Loss rather than an Income Statement. Even though this may confuse the accounting professional and accounting student, it

resonates with the small business user that uses QBO. This report is designed to communicate the revenues earned and expenses incurred for a business over a month, quarter, or year.

Intuit defines this report as follows: "Shows money you earned (income) and money you spent (expenses) so you can see how profitable you are." That is not exactly how an accounting professional or accounting student was taught but close enough. Accountants define the income statement as a report reflecting revenues less expenses to derive net income. Intuit is not about to change its wording to accommodate us, so we will accept it at face value. Thus, revenues are the same as income in the Profit and Loss report. For simplicity, we will refer to this as the Profit and Loss report.

To create a Profit and Loss report for the Sample company, do the following:

1 Open your Internet browser.

2 Type **https://qbo.intuit.com/redir/testdrive** into your browser's address text box, and the press [**Enter**] to view the Sample Company Home page.

3 Click **Reports** from the navigation bar.

4 Type **Profit and Loss** in the Go to report search box and the press [**Enter**].

5 Click the **Collapse** button to provide a more summarized version to view the report shown in Figure 10.1.

Figure 10.1

Profit and Loss report (collapsed and partial views)

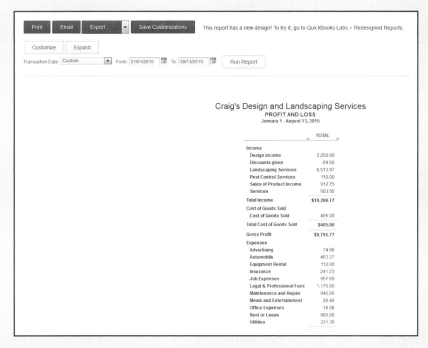

You recall that when using the Sample Company, dates change based upon the system date of Intuit's servers on which these data reside. The system date was 8/13/15 when this report was created; therefore, the default dates for this report were 1/1/15 to 8/13/15 as seen in the From: and To: text boxes at the top of Figure 10.1.

6 Type **1/31/15** in the To: text box, and click **Run Report** to view the report shown in Figure 10.2. (If you are doing this work in a different year, 2016, for example, type 1/31/16.)

Craig's Design and Landscaping Services
PROFIT AND LOSS
January 2015

Income	
Total Income	
Gross Profit	
Expenses	
Total Expenses	
Net Operating Income	
Net Income	

This report contains no data.

Figure 10.2

Profit and Loss report
(for January)

7 The report contains no data because no business events were recorded in that month. Type **7/1/15** (or a beginning of month date where your Sample Company contains the most transactions) in the From: text box and **7/31/15** (or the end of the month date you specified as the beginning of the month date) in the To: text box, and click **Run Report** to view the report shown in Figure 10.3.

Figure 10.3

Profit and Loss report (for July)

Craig's Design and Landscaping Services
PROFIT AND LOSS
July 2015

	TOTAL
Income	
Design income	1,275.00
Discounts given	-89.50
Landscaping Services	4,324.08
Pest Control Services	-30.00
Sales of Product Income	912.75
Services	503.55
Total Income	**$6,895.88**
Cost of Goods Sold	
Cost of Goods Sold	405.00
Total Cost of Goods Sold	**$405.00**
Gross Profit	**$6,490.88**
Expenses	
Advertising	74.86
Automobile	312.81
Equipment Rental	112.00
Insurance	241.23
Job Expenses	602.63
Legal & Professional Fees	565.00
Maintenance and Repair	940.00
Meals and Entertainment	28.49
Office Expenses	18.08
Rent or Lease	900.00
Utilities	188.45
Total Expenses	**$3,983.55**
Net Operating Income	**$2,507.33**
Other Expenses	
Miscellaneous	2,666.00
Total Other Expenses	**$2,666.00**
Net Other Income	**$ -2,666.00**
Net Income	**$ -158.67**

Trouble? If you are doing this work in a different year, 2016, for example, you may have to type a different year and a different month to view the data.

The best way to address this issue is to first generate a Transaction List by Date report like you've done before and selecting **All Dates** as the Transaction Date. The report generated will help you identify what period transactions have been recorded. You should then select a month or accounting period which shows the most transactions.

By defining the accounting period as you did above for the month of July, the only events reported are those recorded during that period. All reports in QBO allow you to drill down to specific transactions recorded in that period. You drill down by clicking an account on a report. That reveals a transactions report for that account for that period. Double-clicking a specific transaction in the transactions report reveals a specific source document such as an invoice, sales receipt, cash receipt, bill, etc. Recall the Trouble? above. The amounts you are asked to investigate below will most likely be different than stated in the steps. Remember you're just using the Sample Company to explore. You will not find these issues in the end-of-chapter case problems.

8 Click the **1,275.00** amount (or whatever amount is shown) next to the Design income account as shown in Figure 10.3 to view the Transaction report for the Design Income account for the month of July shown in Figure 10.4.

Figure 10.4

Transaction Report (for the design income account in July)

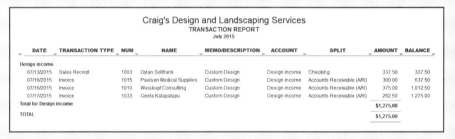

9 Click on the **Dylan Sollfrank** sales receipt to view Sales Receipt #1003 shown in Figure 10.5.

Figure 10.5

Sales Receipt #1003

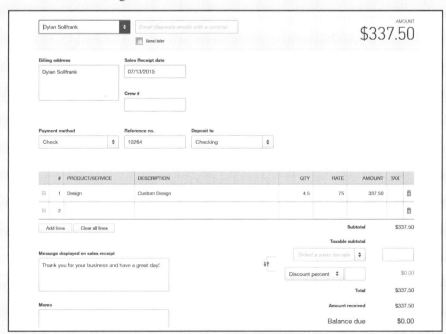

10 Click **Cancel** to return to the transaction report, and click **Back to Summary Report** to return to the Profit and Loss report.

Balance Sheet

In this section, you will create a balance sheet that reports on your company's assets, liabilities, and stockholders' equity as of a specific date (not period). However, when creating this report, QBO provides you the ability to define the period in which underlying account balances will reflect in their transactions reports. QBO default is this Year-to-date. Recall the **Trouble?** above. The amounts you are asked to investigate below will most likely be different than stated in the steps. Remember you're just using the Sample Company to explore. You will not find these issues in the end-of-chapter case problems.

To create a balance sheet, do the following:

1 Continue from where you left off. If you closed the Sample Company, follow the steps to re-open it found at the beginning of this chapter.

2 Click **Reports** from the navigation bar.

3 Type **Balance Sheet** in the Go to report search box, and press [**Enter**] to view the partial balance sheet shown in Figure 10.6.

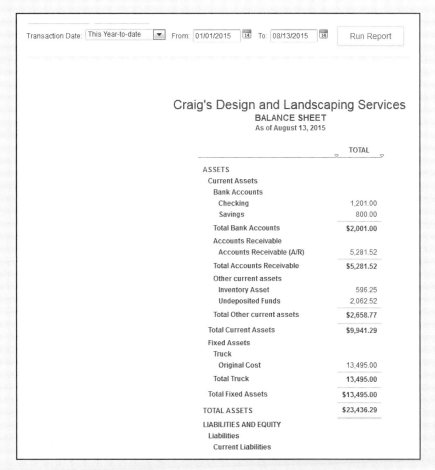

Figure 10.6

Balance Sheet (partial view)

4 The system date in this report is shown as 8/13/15; your date will differ. Type **7/1/15** (or a beginning of month date where your Sample Company contains the most transactions) in the From: date text box, type **7/31/15** (or the end of the month date you specified as the beginning of the month date) in the To: date text box, and click **Run Report** to view the partial

Balance Sheet shown in Figure 10.7. (You may have to type a different month and/or year to view a particular month end Balance Sheet report depending on the report date you are requesting.)

Figure 10.7

Balance Sheet (as of 7/31/15: partial view)

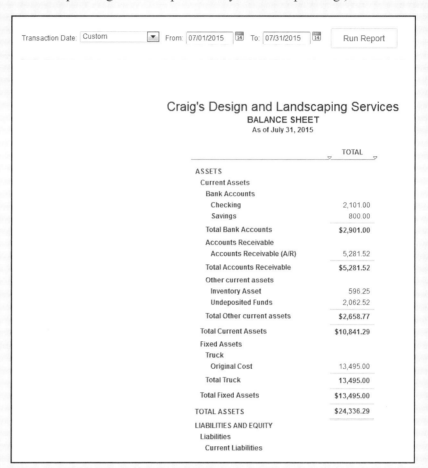

5 Click the Accounts Receivable (A/R) balance that, as shown in Figure 10.7, is **5,281.52** (or whatever balance is shown for Accounts Receivable) to view a transaction report for Accounts Receivable (A/R) for the month of July (or whatever month you selected) shown in Figure 10.8. (Your balance may differ.)

Figure 10.8

Transaction Report (for Accounts Receivable (A/R) for July: partial view)

Craig's Design and Landscaping Services
TRANSACTION REPORT
July 2015

DATE	TRANSACTION TYPE	NUM	NAME	MEMO/DESCRIPTION	ACCOUNT	SPLIT	AMOUNT	BALANCE
Accounts Receivable (A/R)								
Beginning Balance								2,174.00
07/01/2015	Credit Memo	1026	Amy's Bird Sanctuary		Accounts Receivable (A/R)	Pest Control Services	-100.00	2,074.00
07/01/2015	Payment		Amy's Bird Sanctuary		Accounts Receivable (A/R)	-Split-	0.00	2,074.00
07/02/2015	Invoice	1017	Sushi by Katsuyuki		Accounts Receivable (A/R)	Landscaping Services	80.00	2,154.00
07/04/2015	Invoice	1012	Shara Barnett Barnett Design		Accounts Receivable (A/R)	-Split-	274.50	2,428.50
07/06/2015	Invoice	1004	Cool Cars		Accounts Receivable (A/R)	-Split-	2,369.52	4,798.02
07/06/2015	Invoice	1013	Travis Waldron		Accounts Receivable (A/R)	-Split-	81.00	4,879.02

6 Scroll to the end of this report to view the ending balance of 5,281.52, which matches the Balance Sheet report shown in Figure 10.9.

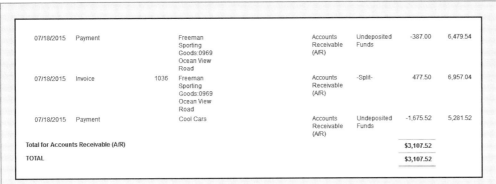

Figure 10.9

Transaction Report end (for Accounts Receivable for July)

7 Click **-1.675.52**, which is the last transaction shown (a payment from Cool Cars) to view the receive payment window shown in Figure 10.10.

Figure 10.10

Payment Received (from Cool Cars)

8 Click **Cancel** to return to the transaction report, and click **Back to Summary Report** to return to the Balance Sheet.

Statement of Cash Flows

In this section, you will create a statement of cash flows, which reports on a company's operating, investing, and financing activities.   Recall the **Trouble?** above. The amounts you are asked to investigate below will most likely be different than stated in the steps. Remember you're just using the Sample Company to explore. You will not find these issues in the end-of-chapter case problems.

To create a statement of cash flows, do the following:

1 Continue from where you left off. If you closed the Sample Company, follow the steps to re-open it found at the beginning of this chapter.

2 Click **Reports** from the navigation bar.

3 Type **Statement of Cash Flows** in the Go to report search box, and press **[Enter]** to view the partial statement of cash flows shown in Figure 10.11.

Figure 10.11

Statement of Cash Flows

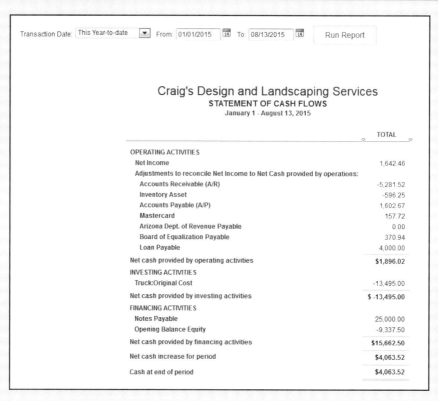

4   The system date in this report is shown as 8/13/15; your date will differ. Type **7/1/15** in the From: date text box, type **7/31/15** in the To: date text box, and click **Run Report** to view the Statement of Cash Flows shown in Figure 10.12. (You may have to type a different month and/or year

Figure 10.12

Statement of Cash Flows (for July)

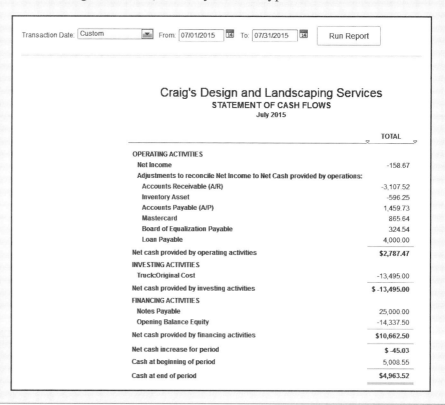

to view a particular month end Statement of Cash Flows report depending on the report date you are requesting.)

5   Click the Notes Payable balance that, as shown in Figure 10.12, is **25,000.00** to view a transaction report for Notes Payable for July shown in Figure 10.13. (Your balance may differ.)

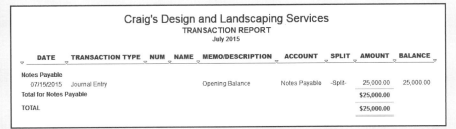

Figure 10.13

Transaction Report (for notes payable for July)

6   Click **25,000.00** to view the journal entry shown in Figure 10.14.

Figure 10.14

Journal date (entry to record the notes payable opening balance)

Journal date			Journal no.	
07/15/2015				

	#	ACCOUNT	DEBITS	CREDITS	DESCRIPTION
⠿	1	Notes Payable		25,000.00	Opening Balance
⠿	2	Opening Balance Equity	25,000.00		Opening Balance

7   Click **Cancel** to return to the transaction report, and click **Back to Summary Report** to return to the Statement of Cash Flows.

Accounts Receivable Aging Summary

In this section, you will create an accounts receivable aging summary, which reflects unpaid invoices for the current period and for the last 30, 60 and 90+ days as of a specific date. Aging summaries help find customers who may be delinquent in their payments and help a company estimate the need for an allowance for uncollectible accounts. Aging information must take into consideration the company's normal terms for a customer. For example, it would not be an issue if many customers are in the 60+ category, but the normal terms for those customers are net 60. However, it would be an issue if the normal terms are net 30 and the same situation existed. Recall the **Trouble?** above. The amounts you are asked to investigate below will most likely be different than stated in the steps. Remember you're just using the Sample Company to explore. You will not find these issues in the end-of-chapter case problems.

To create an accounts receivable aging summary report, do the following:

1   Continue from where you left off. If you closed the Sample Company, follow the steps to re-open it found at the beginning of this chapter.

2   Click **Reports** from the navigation bar.

3   Type **A/R Aging Summary** in the Go to report search box, and press [**Enter**] to view the accounts receivable (A/R) aging report shown in Figure 10.15.

Figure 10.15

Accounts Receivable (A/R) Aging
Summary

Craig's Design and Landscaping Services
A/R AGING SUMMARY
As of August 13, 2015

	CURRENT	1 - 30	31 - 60	61 - 90	91 AND OVER	TOTAL
Amy's Bird Sanctuary		239.00				$239.00
Bill's Windsurf Shop			85.00			$85.00
Freeman Sporting Goods						$0.00
0969 Ocean View Road	477.50					$477.50
55 Twin Lane		4.00	81.00			$85.00
Total Freeman Sporting Goods	477.50	4.00	81.00	0.00	0.00	$562.50
Geeta Kalapatapu	629.10					$629.10
Jeff's Jalopies		81.00				$81.00
John Melton		450.00				$450.00
Kookies by Kathy			75.00			$75.00
Mark Cho	314.28					$314.28
Paulsen Medical Supplies	954.75					$954.75
Red Rock Diner	70.00			156.00		$226.00
Rondonuwu Fruit and Vegi	78.60					$78.60
Shara Barnett						$0.00
Barnett Design		274.50				$274.50
Total Shara Barnett	0.00	274.50	0.00	0.00	0.00	$274.50
Sonnenschein Family Store	362.07					$362.07
Sushi by Katsuyuki	80.00	80.00				$160.00
Travis Waldron	414.72					$414.72
Weiskopf Consulting	375.00					$375.00
TOTAL	$3,756.02	$1,128.50	$241.00	$156.00	$0.00	$5,281.52

4   The system date in this report is shown as 8/13/15; your date will differ. (You may have to type a different month and/or year to view a particular month end A/R Aging report depending on the report date you are requesting.)

5   Click on the **85.00** owed by Bill's Windsurf Shop shown in Figure 10.15 to view A/R Aging Detail report shown in Figure 10.16.

Figure 10.16

Accounts Receivable (A/R) Aging
Detail Report

Craig's Design and Landscaping Services
A/R AGING DETAIL
As of August 13, 2015

DATE	TRANSACTION TYPE	NUM	CLIENT	DUE DATE	AMOUNT	OPEN BALANCE
31 - 60 days past due						
05/31/2015 Invoice		1027	Bill's Windsurf Shop	06/30/2015	85.00	85.00
Total for 31 - 60 days past due					$85.00	$85.00
TOTAL					$85.00	$85.00

6   Click **85.00** to view invoice #1027 shown in Figure 10.17.

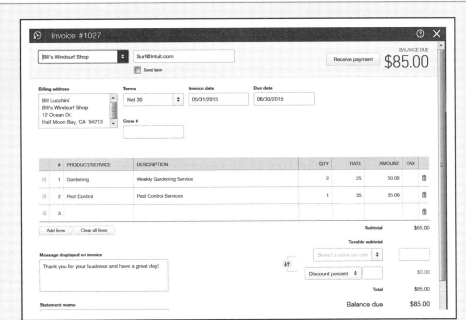

Figure 10.17

Invoice #1027
(to Bill's Windsurf Shop)

7 Call Bill to find out when he is planning to pay you. Actually, no, do not do that. Instead, click **Cancel** to return to the detail report, and click **Back to Summary Report** to return to the A/R Aging Summary report.

Accounts Payable Aging Summary

In this section, you will create an accounts payable aging summary, which reflects unpaid bills for the current period and for the last 30, 60, and 90+ days as of a specific date. Aging summaries help prioritize the payment of bills. Aging information must take into consideration the company's normal terms from a vendor. For example, it would not be an issue if a large amount of vendors bills are in the 60+ category, but the normal terms for those vendors are net 60. However, it would be an issue if the normal terms are net 30, and the same situation existed. Recall the **Trouble?** above. The amounts you are asked to investigate below will most likely be different than stated in the steps. Remember you're just using the Sample Company to explore. You will not find these issues in the end-of-chapter case problems.

To create an accounts payable aging summary report, do the following:

1 Continue from where you left off. If you closed the Sample Company, follow the steps to re-open it found at the beginning of this chapter.

2 Click **Reports** from the navigation bar.

3 Type **A/P Aging Summary** in the Go to report search box, and press **[Enter]** to view the accounts payable aging report shown in Figure 10.18.

4 The system date in this report is shown as 8/13/15; your date will differ. (You may have to type a different month and/or year to view a particular month end A/P Aging report depending on the report date you are requesting.)

5   Click on the **86.44** owed to PG&E shown in Figure 10.18 to view A/P Aging Detail report shown in Figure 10.19.

Figure 10.18

Accounts Payable (A/P) Aging Summary

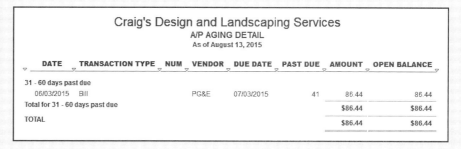

6   Click **86.44** to view the bill shown in Figure 10.20.

Figure 10.19

Accounts Payable (A/P) Aging Detail Report

Figure 10.20

Bill (from PG&E)

7   Write a check to PG&E before the power gets cut off. Actually, no, do not do that. Instead, click **Cancel** to return to the detail report, and click **Back to Summary Report** to return to the A/P Aging Summary report.

Inventory Valuation Summary

In this section, you will create an inventory valuation summary that reflects each inventory item's quantity on hand, its average cost, and the resulting valuation as of a specific date. Recall the **Trouble?** above. The amounts you are asked to investigate below will most likely be different than stated in the steps. Remember you're just using the Sample Company to explore. You will not find these issues in the end-of-chapter case problems.

To create an inventory valuation summary report, do the following:

1   Continue from where you left off. If you closed the Sample Company, follow the steps to re-open it found at the beginning of this chapter.

2   Click **Reports** from the navigation bar.

3   Type **Inventory Valuation Summary** in the Go to report search box, and press [**Enter**] to view the inventory valuation summary report shown in Figure 10.21.

Craig's Design and Landscaping Services
INVENTORY VALUATION SUMMARY
As of August 13, 2015

	QTY	ASSET VALUE	AVG COST
		TOTAL	
Pump	25.00	250.00	10.00
Rock Fountain	2.00	250.00	125.00
Sprinkler Heads	25.00	18.75	0.75
Sprinkler Pipes	31.00	77.50	2.50
TOTAL		$596.25	

Figure 10.21

Inventory Valuation Summary

4   The system date in this report is shown as 8/13/15; your date will differ. (You may have to type a different month and/or year to view a particular month end Inventory Valuation Summary report depending on the report date you are requesting.)

5   Click on the **25** representing the number of pumps on hand shown in Figure 10.21 to view an Inventory Valuation Detail report shown in Figure 10.22.

Craig's Design and Landscaping Services
INVENTORY VALUATION DETAIL
As of August 13, 2015

DATE	TRANSACTION TYPE	NUM	QTY	QUANTITY	AVG COST	RATE	ASSET VALUE
Pump							
07/18/2015	Check	75	3.00	3.00	10.00	10.00	30.00
07/18/2015	Inventory Qty Adjust	START	16.00	19.00	10.00	10.00	190.00
07/18/2015	Invoice	1036	-1.00	18.00	10.00	10.00	180.00
07/18/2015	Bill		8.00	26.00	10.00	10.00	260.00
07/18/2015	Invoice	1037	-1.00	25.00	10.00	10.00	250.00

Figure 10.22

Inventory Valuation Detail

6   Click **Bill** reflecting the purchase of eight pumps shown in Figure 10.22 to view the bill shown in Figure 10.23.

Figure 10.23

Bill (from Norton Lumber for the purchase of eight pumps)

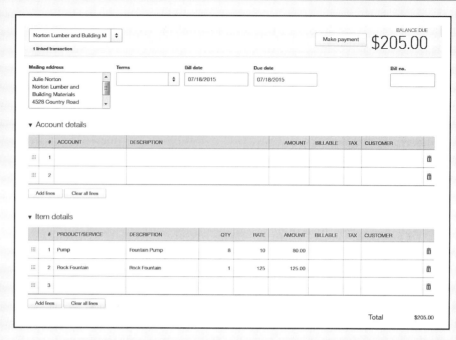

7   Click **Cancel** to return to the detail report, and click **Back to Summary Report** to return to the A/P Aging Summary report.

Customizing and Saving Reports

All of the reports available in QBO can be customized in some fashion and saved for later use. In this section, you will customize a Profit and Loss report as an example. Recall the **Trouble?** above. The amounts you are asked to investigate below will most likely be different than stated in the steps. Remember you're just using the Sample Company to explore. You will not find these issues in the end-of-chapter case problems.

To customize and save a Profit and Loss report, do the following:

1   Continue from where you left off. If you closed the Sample Company, follow the steps to re-open it found at the beginning of this chapter.

2   Click **Reports** from the navigation bar.

3   Type **Profit and Loss** in the Go to report search box and press [**Enter**].

4   Click **Collapse**.

5   Type **6/1/15** in the From: date text box and **7/31/15** in the To: date text box, and click **Run Report** to view the Profit and Loss report shown in Figure 10.24.

Figure 10.24

Profit and Loss report (for June to July 2015)

Craig's Design and Landscaping Services
PROFIT AND LOSS
June - July, 2015

	TOTAL
Income	
Design income	2,250.00
Discounts given	-89.50
Landscaping Services	4,879.72
Pest Control Services	-30.00
Sales of Product Income	912.75
Services	503.55
Total Income	**$8,426.52**
Cost of Goods Sold	
Cost of Goods Sold	405.00
Total Cost of Goods Sold	**$405.00**
Gross Profit	**$8,021.52**
Expenses	
Advertising	74.86
Automobile	374.82
Equipment Rental	112.00
Insurance	241.23
Job Expenses	799.81
Legal & Professional Fees	620.00
Maintenance and Repair	940.00
Meals and Entertainment	28.49
Office Expenses	18.08
Rent or Lease	900.00
Utilities	331.39
Total Expenses	**$4,440.68**
Net Operating Income	**$3,580.84**
Other Expenses	
Miscellaneous	2,916.00
Total Other Expenses	**$2,916.00**
Net Other Income	**$ -2,916.00**
Net Income	**$664.84**

6   Click **Customize**, and select **Months** from the Columns drop-down list in the Rows/Columns section of the Customize Profit and Loss window shown in Figure 10.25.

Figure 10.25

Customize Profit and Loss report

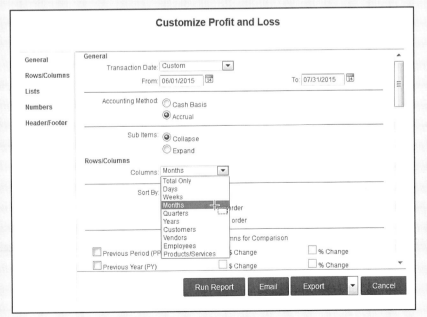

7 Scroll down the Customize Profit and Loss window, and place a check in the **% of Income** check box.

8 Click **Run Report** to view the customized Profit and Loss report shown in Figure 10.26.

Figure 10.26

Profit and Loss report (customized version)

Craig's Design and Landscaping Services
PROFIT AND LOSS
June - July, 2015

	JUN 2015		JUL 2015		TOTAL	
	CURRENT	% OF INCOME	CURRENT	% OF INCOME	CURRENT	% OF INCOME
Income						
Design income	975.00	63.70 %	1,275.00	18.49 %	$2,250.00	26.70 %
Discounts given			-89.50	-1.30 %	$ -89.50	-1.06 %
Landscaping Services	555.64	36.30 %	4,324.08	62.71 %	$4,879.72	57.91 %
Pest Control Services			-30.00	-0.44 %	$ -30.00	-0.36 %
Sales of Product Income			912.75	13.24 %	$912.75	10.83 %
Services			503.55	7.30 %	$503.55	5.98 %
Total Income	**$1,530.64**	**100.00 %**	**$6,895.88**	**100.00 %**	**$8,426.52**	**100.00 %**
Cost of Goods Sold						
Cost of Goods Sold			405.00	5.87 %	$405.00	4.81 %
Total Cost of Goods Sold	**$0.00**	**0.00%**	**$405.00**	**5.87 %**	**$405.00**	**4.81 %**
Gross Profit	**$1,530.64**	**100.00 %**	**$6,490.88**	**94.13 %**	**$8,021.52**	**95.19 %**
Expenses						
Advertising			74.86	1.09 %	$74.86	0.89 %
Automobile	62.01	4.05 %	312.81	4.54 %	$374.82	4.45 %
Equipment Rental			112.00	1.62 %	$112.00	1.33 %
Insurance			241.23	3.50 %	$241.23	2.86 %
Job Expenses	197.18	12.88 %	602.63	8.74 %	$799.81	9.49 %
Legal & Professional Fees	55.00	3.59 %	565.00	8.19 %	$620.00	7.36 %
Maintenance and Repair			940.00	13.63 %	$940.00	11.16 %
Meals and Entertainment			28.49	0.41 %	$28.49	0.34 %
Office Expenses			18.08	0.26 %	$18.08	0.21 %
Rent or Lease			900.00	13.05 %	$900.00	10.68 %
Utilities	142.94	9.34 %	188.45	2.73 %	$331.39	3.93 %
Total Expenses	**$457.13**	**29.87 %**	**$3,983.55**	**57.77 %**	**$4,440.68**	**52.70 %**
Net Operating Income	**$1,073.51**	**70.13%**	**$2,507.33**	**36.36 %**	**$3,580.84**	**42.49 %**
Other Expenses						
Miscellaneous	250.00	16.33 %	2,666.00	38.66 %	$2,916.00	34.61 %
Total Other Expenses	**$250.00**	**16.33 %**	**$2,666.00**	**38.66 %**	**$2,916.00**	**34.61 %**
Net Other Income	**$ -250.00**	**-16.33 %**	**$ -2,666.00**	**-38.66 %**	**$ -2,916.00**	**-34.61 %**
Net Income	**$823.51**	**53.80 %**	**$ -158.67**	**-2.30 %**	**$664.84**	**7.89 %**

9 Click **Save Customizations**.

10 Type **Profit and Loss Comparison** as the new name for this report, and share it as you have done in previous chapters.

End Note

In this chapter, you did not add business events, but you did create the basic financial statement reports: profit and loss, balance sheet, and statement of cash flows. In addition, you drilled down beyond those reports to transaction detail reports and to source documents like payments, invoices, bills, etc. You created some analytical reports to learn more about accounts receivable, accounts payable, and inventory. Lastly, you learned how to customize reports and save those reports for later use.

Chapter 10 Questions

View the sample company QBO file to answer these questions by creating reports:

1 Invoice 1015 was created for which customer?

2 What was the first item on sold on invoice 1015?

3 What was the last item sold that was categorized as sales of product income?

4 Who sent a bill for $315.00 in accounting fees?

5 How many sprinkler head are currently on hand?

6 What is the average cost per unit of sprinkler heads?

7 Who is the most delinquent customer?

8 What is the total amount of receivables that are current?

9 What amount of payables are 1–30 days past due?

10 What amount of cash was provided by financing activities?

Chapter 10 Matching

a. Income statement

b. Balance sheet

c. Statement of cash flows

d. AR aging report

e. AP aging report

f. Inventory valuation report

g. Profit and loss report

h. To view a transaction report

i. To view a source document

j. % of income check box

_____ Click on an event in any transaction report

_____ Click an account on any report

_____ Click to add a new column in a report

_____ Reflects unpaid bills for the current period

_____ Reports revenues and expenses

_____ Includes operating, investing, and financing activities

_____ Reports inventory quantities on hand

_____ Reports assets, liabilities, and equities

_____ Another name for the income statement

_____ Reflects unpaid invoices for the current period

Chapter 10 Cases

The following cases require you to open the company you updated in Chapter 9. Each case below continues throughout the text in a sequential manner. Each case below is similar in concepts assessed but differ in amounts and transactions.

To reopen your company, do the following:

1 Open your Internet browser.

2 Type **https://qbo.intuit.com/qbo28/login?webredir** into your browser's address text box.

3 Type your User ID and Password into the text boxes as you have before.

Case 1

Based on what you learned in the chapter and using the Sample Company, you are to create the following reports for your company continuing from Chapter 9:

1 Create, print, and export to Excel a Profit and Loss report for January 2018. Customize this report by adding a percent of income column and saving and by sharing your customization as Profit and Loss Jan 2018.

2 Using the Profit and Loss report created above, drill down to a Transactions Report for the Sales account. Print and export this report to Excel. Save and share this report as a Sales Transaction Report.

3 Create, print, and export to Excel a Balance Sheet report as of 1/31/18. Customize this report by adding a percent of column column and saving and sharing your customization as Balance Sheet Jan 2018.

4 Using the Balance Sheet report created above, drill down to a Transactions Report for the Checking account. Print and export this report to Excel. Save and share this report as Checking Report.

5 Create, print, and export to Excel a Statement of Cash Flows report as of 1/31/18. Save and share your customization as Statement of Cash Flows Jan 2018.

6 Using the Statement of Cash Flows report created above, drill down to a Transactions Report for the Accounts Receivable account. Print and export this report to Excel. Save and share this report as an A/R SCF Report.

7 Create, print, and export to Excel an A/R Aging Summary report for the month of January 2018. Save and share your customization as A/R Aging Summary Jan 2018.

8 Create, print, and export to Excel an A/P Aging Summary report for the month of January 2018. Save and share your customization as A/P Aging Summary Jan 2018

9 Create, print, and export to Excel an Inventory Valuation Summary report for the month of January 2018. Save and share your customization as an Inventory Valuation Summary Jan 2018

Case 2

Based on what you learned in the chapter and using the Sample Company, you are to create the following reports for your company continuing from Chapter 9:

1 Create, print, and export to Excel a Profit and Loss report for January 2019. Customize this report by adding a percent of income column. Save and share your customization as Profit and Loss Jan 2019.

2 Using the Profit and Loss report created above, drill down to a Transactions Report for the Insurance account. Print and export this report to Excel. Save and share this report as an Insurance Transaction Report.

3 Create, print, and export to Excel a Balance Sheet report as of 1/31/19. Customize this report by adding a percent of column column. Save and share your customization as Balance Sheet Jan 2019.

4 Using the Balance Sheet report created above, drill down to a Transactions Report for the Inventory Asset account. Print and export this report to Excel. Save and share this report as Inventory Report.

5 Create, print, and export to Excel a Statement of Cash Flows report as of 1/31/19. Save and share your customization as Statement of Cash Flows Jan 2019.

6 Using the Statement of Cash Flows report created above, drill down to a Transactions Report for the Prepaid Expenses account. Print and export this report to Excel. Save and share this report as PPE SCF Report.

7 Create, print, and export to Excel an A/R Aging Summary report for the month of January 2019. Save and share your customization as an A/R Aging Summary Jan 2019.

8 Create, print, and export to Excel an A/P Aging Summary report for the month of January 2019. Save and share your customization as an A/P Aging Summary Jan 2019.

9 Create, print, and export to Excel an Inventory Valuation Summary report for January 2018. Save and share your customization as Inventory Valuation Summary Jan 2018.

index

Notes

Notes

Notes

Notes

Notes

Notes

Notes